A Passion for Stea
Settle & Carlisle Line

Above: London Midland and Scottish Railway (LMS) Princess Royal Class No 46203 *Princess Margaret Rose* was a regular performer over the Settle and Carlisle in the 1990's. Here on 20 August 1994 she departs Appleby in fine style with a southbound Cumbrian Mountain Express.

Right: A firm favourite with all enthusiasts in the 1980s was the National railway museum Duchess Class No 46229 *Duchess of Hamilton*. Here she powers through Dent station with a southbound Cumbrian Mountain Express.

Front cover and previous page: The first passing of LNER 'Pacifics' on the Settle & Carlisle line in the preservation era were seen on 11 September 1993. Thanks to the cooperation of the A4 Locomotive Society, the author was able to capture this remarkable image from the footplate of 'A4' 'Pacific' No 4498 Sir Nigel Gresley as it descended from Ais Gill just as Peppercorn 'A2' 'Pacific' No 60532 Blue Peter climbed away from Birkett Tunnel with a southbound 'Cumbrian Mountain Express'.

A Passion for Steam on the Settle & Carlisle Line

Maurice Burns

Silver Link Publishing Ltd

First published in 2018

British Library Cataloguing in Publication Data
A catalogue record for this book is available from the British Library.

Standard Edition ISBN 978185794 534 8
Limited Edition ISBN 978 185794 533 1

Silver Link Publishing Ltd
The Trundle
Ringstead Road
Great Addington
Kettering
Northants NN14 4BW

Tel/Fax: 01536 330588
email: sales@nostalgiacollection.com
Website: www.nostalgiacollection.com

Printed and bound in the Czech Republic

All photographs are by the author unless otherwise credited.

Acknowledgements

The author would like to thank all those who have supported this book project and share my passion for the Settle & Carlisle Railway. These include lifelong friends Ted Parker, Dave Whitfield, Brian Nun, Nick Carter, Geoff Scurr, Garth McLean and John Emmerson.

While the majority of the photographs are my own, I would like to thank those, mentioned in the photo credits, who have allowed some of their images to appear in this book. Thanks must also go to David Dunn and Richard Barber of the Armstrong Railway Photographic Trust for help with scanning my photographic collection, and also to Steve Edge for kindly producing the maps.

Special thanks must go to David Ward, who for many years was responsible for main-line steam and is now a Vice President of The Friends of the Settle & Carlisle Line, for agreeing to do the Foreword for this book. Also thanks to those who have assisted in the proofreading, including Mary Kinneavy, and Will Adams.

Finally thanks must go to Val, my daughter Pam and son Graham, who supported me in my efforts in the steam preservation movement with NELPG that allowed me to be involved in so many locomotive restorations, including returning 'K1' 2-6-0 No 2005 and 'A2' 'Pacific' No 60532 *Blue Peter* to main-line condition, both of which have operated successfully over the Settle to Carlisle line.

The author is hoping in future years to produce further books in the Passion for steam series to cover the North East and Scotland and would appreciate any feedback on this his first book to maurice_burns2000@yahoo.com.

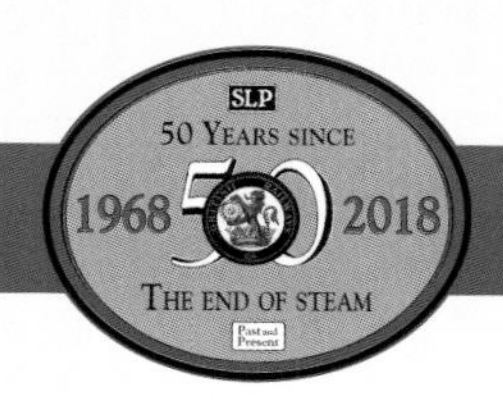

Contents

The Settle & Carlisle Line

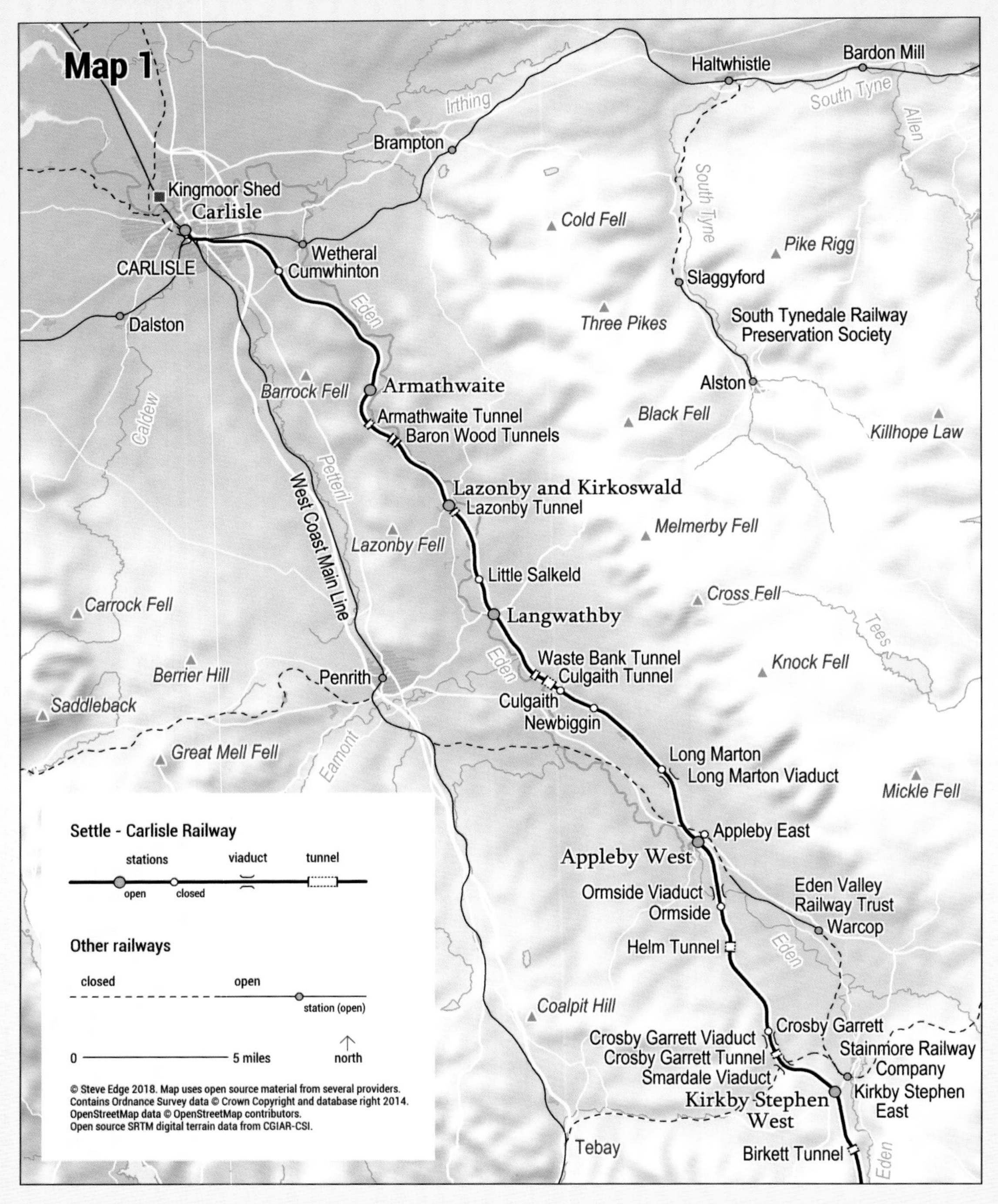

Route Map

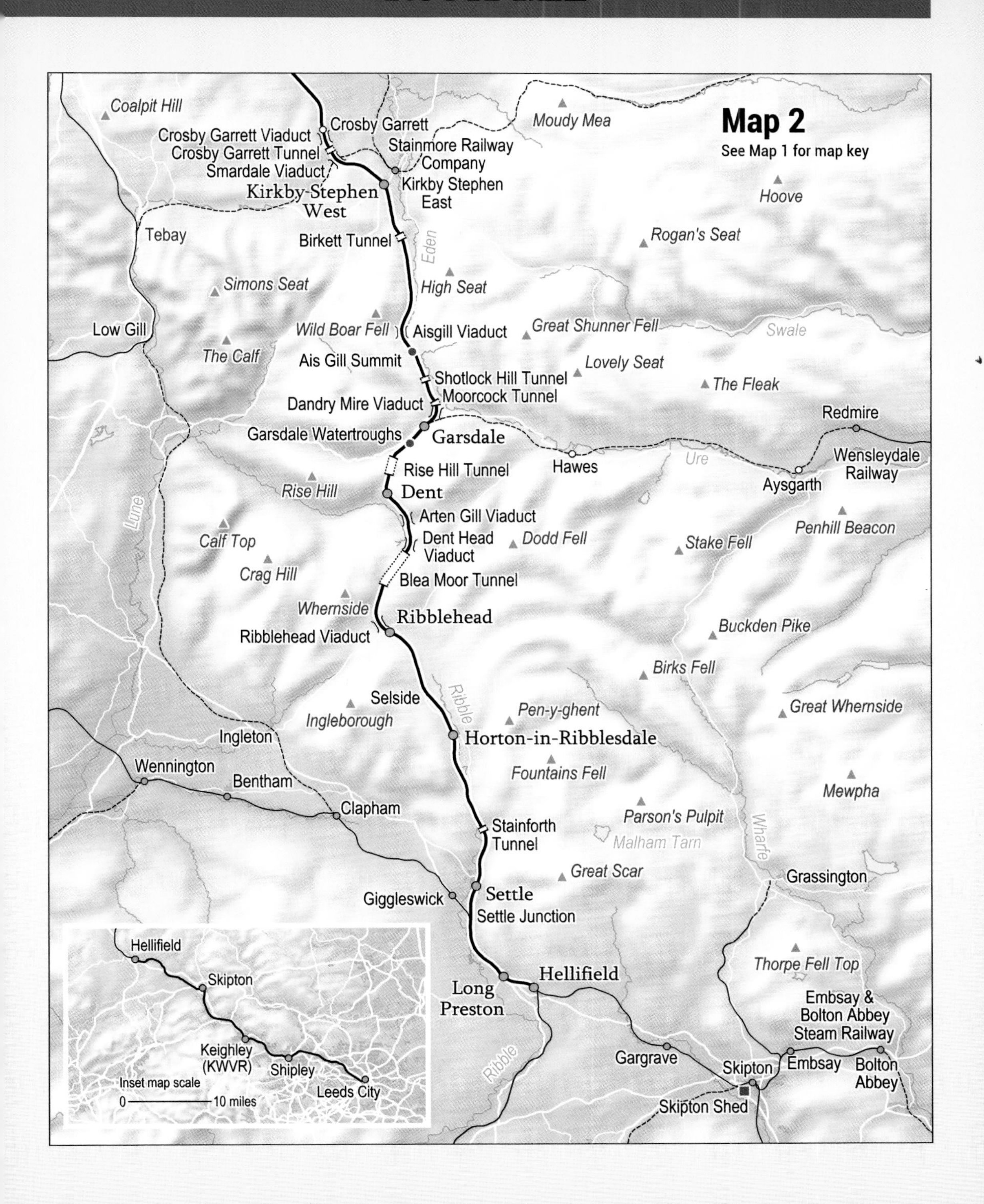
Map 2
See Map 1 for map key
Coalpit Hill
Crosby Garrett
Crosby Garrett Viaduct
Crosby Garrett Tunnel
Smardale Viaduct
Stainmore Railway Company
Moudy Mea
Kirkby-Stephen West
Kirkby Stephen East
Hoove
Tebay
Birkett Tunnel
Eden
Rogan's Seat
Simons Seat
High Seat
Low Gill
Wild Boar Fell
Aisgill Viaduct
Great Shunner Fell
Swale
The Calf
Ais Gill Summit
Shotlock Hill Tunnel
Lovely Seat
The Fleak
Dandry Mire Viaduct
Moorcock Tunnel
Redmire
Garsdale Watertroughs
Garsdale
Hawes
Ure
Wensleydale Railway
Rise Hill Tunnel
Aysgarth
Rise Hill
Dent
Lune
Arten Gill Viaduct
Penhill Beacon
Calf Top
Dent Head Viaduct
Dodd Fell
Stake Fell
Crag Hill
Blea Moor Tunnel
Whernside
Ribblehead
Buckden Pike
Ribblehead Viaduct
Birks Fell
Selside
Ribble
Pen-y-ghent
Great Whernside
Ingleborough
Ingleton
Horton-in-Ribblesdale
Wennington
Bentham
Fountains Fell
Mewpha
Clapham
Parson's Pulpit
Stainforth Tunnel
Malham Tarn
Wharfe
Great Scar
Grassington
Giggleswick
Settle
Settle Junction
Thorpe Fell Top
Hellifield
Long Preston
Embsay & Bolton Abbey Steam Railway
Gargrave
Skipton
Embsay
Bolton Abbey
Skipton Shed
Hellifield
Skipton
Keighley (KWVR)
Shipley
Leeds City
Inset map scale
0 10 miles

FOREWORD by David Ward

Vice President of The Friends of The Settle & Carlisle Line

This book is a must-have for all those interested in railways and in particular the Settle to Carlisle railway line, the last ten years of steam operation on BR, and the remarkable renaissance of steam locomotive operation on the main line by privately preserved steam locomotives. It is a record told by Maurice Burns who was intimately present or involved throughout 60 years from 1958 to 2018, and it is supported by images taken at the time and therefore represents an accurate history. One can only marvel at the dedicated interest and energy of the author in cycling over 100 miles most weekends to obtain well-planned photographs and such a wealth of records on what is perhaps the best-loved and most famous railway line in England.

The author was one of those dozen or so practical engineers who initiated the practice of acquiring and overhauling withdrawn main-line steam locomotives to a standard acceptable to operate special trains on BR main lines. This was an enormous achievement requiring not only engineering skills and business acumen but also the ability to work with and learn from professional railwaymen. It also required working to the limit of personal sacrifice both in time and money. The author can therefore write with authority on this subject, and the photographs show the very high standards achieved.

The book also contains stories and images of visits to other lines in the North West now long since closed, and these also provide an invaluable record.

Above all, the book is the life story of a man's hobby, which has not only given him much pleasure but has also considerably added to the pleasure of the millions interested in railways. All those who take pleasure today in seeing or riding behind a steam locomotive on the main line or on private railways owe a great debt of gratitude to Maurice. It would also be correct to say that it is highly probable the Settle to Carlisle line would have closed in 1979 had its public profile and income not been significantly brought to the fore by the operation of trains hauled by preserved steam locomotives.

The combination of words and images provides an indisputable historic record of how it was, and still is, and I commend the book to all those interested in railway history, the steam locomotive and the Settle to Carlisle railway line.

David Ward
July 2018

Introduction

This book is being published to coincide with the 50th anniversary of the last BR steam-hauled train over the Settle & Carlisle Railway – the '15 Guinea Special' of 11 August 1968. It will describe a personal journey through time and the extraordinary efforts to photograph the steam locomotives on the Settle & Carlisle line, both in the final days of British Railways service and in the preservation era, spanning a remarkable period of 50 years.

My life began far away from the beautiful Eden Valley, Dentdale and Ribblehead, in the industrial North East. I was born on the Headland at Hartlepool in County Durham on 25 March 1946, within sight and sound of the sea, coal staithes, fishing boats, riveting guns at the shipyard and of course steam engines! This was a far cry from the Settle & Carlisle line on the other side of the Pennines, but as my parents loved the outdoors and mountain-climbing it was not long before as a young boy I was going with them over to the Lake District, climbing Great Gable, Helvellyn and Blencathra and crossing the S&C at Appleby.

My relatives were all involved in heavy engineering and my father was no exception, starting his working life as a pattern-maker but going on to much greater things in international contracting, resulting in several house moves. From Hartlepool we moved to Pontefract in Yorkshire, and at the age of 10 we moved to Stockton-on-Tees, then in County Durham. By coincidence our new home was next to the freight-only Teesside to Shildon line, known locally as the 'Cuckoo Line'. This was electrified by Sir Vincent Raven, CME of the North Eastern Railway, to replace steam haulage. However, in later years it reverted to steam haulage and every day there would be a procession of coal trains hauled by North Eastern Railway 'Q6s'.

Visiting grandparents at any age is always a treat, especially as one lived next to a railway embankment north of Hartlepool, near Cemetery North signal box. From their back garden I could see signals for both directions, so I even knew when steam was going to pass. Beside all the coal traffic and local passenger trains, there were three expresses with 'namers' such as *Trigo*, *Shotover*, *Sunstar*, *Wilson Worsdell*, *Boswell*, *North Eastern*, *Bronzino*, *Steady Aim*, *Ocean Swell* and *Sugar Palm*, to name but a few. My bedroom faced the railway line and I would stay awake till 11pm looking out into the darkness for the King's Cross sleeper, usually 'A3'-hauled, and watch the glow from the firebox as it passed by, before falling asleep.

At school everyone was a trainspotter and I soon got the bug. When I was just 11 or 12 years old my trusting parents would let me go anywhere by train, perhaps in the belief, as I was in the Scouts, that I would find my way back home! Journeys were first to Northallerton to see the 'A4'-hauled expresses roar through, then further afield to the busy stations at York, Newcastle and Leeds and their associated loco sheds full of steam. Some loco sheds such as York were easily located from the train, but those in Leeds were more difficult and we would wander round the streets of the city to find Holbeck. It was as if a magnet was pulling us, and all other spotters, in the right direction and, once located, we would find the secret way into the loco shed to avoid being caught trespassing, though in reality officialdom was rarely a problem. Loco sheds were of course dangerous places, with moving engines and inspection pits to fall into, but enthusiasts had no need for a safety briefing as they appeared to have, as part of their DNA, a built-in awareness of everything around them and general safety even at the young age of 12. It was on this first visit to Holbeck that I took a picture with a Brownie camera of a steam engine associated with the Settle & Carlisle line. This was immaculate 'Britannia' No 70053 *Moray Firth* being prepared for 'The Thames-Clyde Express'.

The most adventurous journey at the age of 12 was with the aid of a 'Runabout' ticket to Carlisle. Carlisle was just an incredible place with LMS and LNER locomotives departing from the same station. It had four locomotive sheds at that time: Upperby, Canal, Durran Hill and Kingmoor. I was fortunate to take one picture at Durran Hill shed before it closed, of a type of engine I had not seen before – unrebuilt 'Patriot' No 45513. Durran Hill closed soon after on 2 November 1959, with Kingmoor then taking

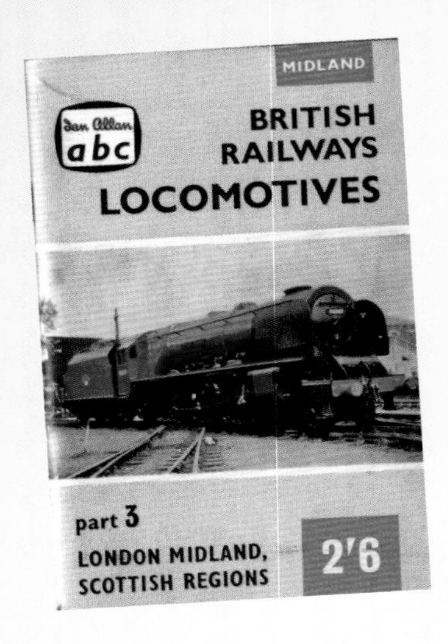

Above: Every trainspotter had to have a copy of the Ian Allan trainspotters book to underline the engines seen. This is Part 3, which covered the London Midland and Scottish Regions, and was produced in the summer of 1959. *Author's collection*

Above right: With only a Brownie camera to record the scene on Leeds Holbeck shed in August 1959, immaculate 'Britannia' No 70053 *Moray Firth*, then allocated to Holbeck, is being prepared for 'The Thames-Clyde Express'.

over responsibility for steam over the S&C.

On my 13th birthday I received my best every present, a bicycle. However, this was no ordinary bicycle but a lightweight hand-built Jack Taylor bicycle, made in my home town of Stockton-on-Tees. This bicycle became part of me and together we could now go anywhere, and that we certainly did. My adventurous spirit, inherited from my father, knew no bounds, with 75-mile rides to Sunderland to see the last 'A8' tanks, a 96-mile trip to Newcastle followed by a 98-mile trip to York. I was becoming acutely aware of steam's decline and the older classes of engines becoming extinct and the need to photograph them – even with just a Brownie camera.

At 14 the first of many cycling holidays took place, covering considerable distances. The first, with fellow cyclist Chris Smith, was to Edinburgh, to be followed, at 15, by a ride over Beattock and Rannoch Moor to Fort William, Inverness, Aberdeen, Dundee and Edinburgh. The longest trip, with another friend, Stephen Brown, was to Killarney in southern Ireland, covering 1,300 miles. All of these trips involved staying in Youth Hostels, something that was great fun and so popular at the time, even if the duties had to be fitted in round the visits to loco sheds!

From time to time I borrowed my father's camera, a British-made 35mm Ilford Advocate, but then bought my first decent camera, a 35mm Practika IV and a 135mm fixed telephoto lens. I had converted the old coal house into a great permanent darkroom, my father being a keen photographer, from the age of eight I had helped him with his printing. Taking the picture was not as easy as it is today, with auto-focus, zoom lenses, electronic flash or multiple pictures per second from which to pick the right frame.

Left: My only picture at Carlisle Durran Hill shed, captured with a Brownie camera, shows unrebuilt, and unnamed Fowler 'Patriot' No 45513 awaiting its next duty. Durran Hill, the original loco shed for the Midland route to Leeds, closed on 2 November 1959.

In the 1960s focusing was manual, as was the exposure after taking a light reading on a Western meter. The hardest thing of all was pressing the shutter at the right time with a fast-moving train – for every action picture it had to be right first time! There was no second chance. Night-time photography was always a challenge, with the use of tripods, cable releases for exposures of many seconds, and Phillips PF5 flashbulbs. When cycling the amount of equipment was heavy, as it included a portable Phillips reel-to-reel tape-recorder, but the heavy weight was the way it was and we knew no different.

On 22 July 1961 myself (left) and friend Chris Smith pose for the camera on our bikes in Barnard Avenue, Stockton-on-Tees, before setting off to Fort William, Inverness, Aberdeen, Dundee and Edinburgh.

Until 1966 the cycle was the mode of transport to reach all parts of the Settle & Carlisle line, and many of the adventures are detailed in this book. The effort of getting there via Wensleydale or Stainmore or cycling over the Coal Road from Garsdale to Dent was never a problem. It was just so incredible to see steam engines hard at work on such a beautiful line.

I started my first job as an apprentice engineering draughtsman and in February 1966 I passed my driving test and was given

Cycling adventures were extensive, and the *Belfast Telegraph* newspaper caught me (left, at 17 years old) with friend Stephen Brown in Belfast as we planned our journey to Killarney in southern Ireland on 21 July 1963.

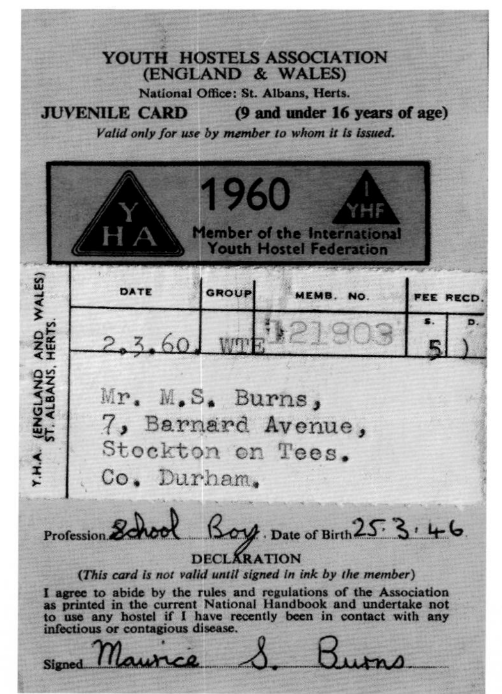

YOUTH HOSTELS ASSOCIATION
(ENGLAND & WALES)
National Office: St. Albans, Herts.
JUVENILE CARD (9 and under 16 years of age)
Valid only for use by member to whom it is issued.

1960
YHA
Member of the International Youth Hostel Federation
IYHF

Y.H.A. (ENGLAND AND WALES) ST. ALBANS, HERTS.

DATE	GROUP	MEMB. NO.	FEE RECD. s.	D.
2.3.60	WTE	121903	5	)

Mr. M.S. Burns,
7, Barnard Avenue,
Stockton on Tees.
Co. Durham.

Profession School Boy Date of Birth 25.3.46

DECLARATION
(This card is not valid until signed in ink by the member)
I agree to abide by the rules and regulations of the Association as printed in the current National Handbook and undertake not to use any hostel if I have recently been in contact with any infectious or contagious disease.

Signed Maurice S. Burns

All the trips away from home involved staying at Youth Hostels. Here is my Juvenile membership card for 1960, when my profession was still 'school boy'!

my Mum's 10-year-old Ford Consul. This made trips to the Settle & Carlisle easier although, with limited income, money was tight.

The pictures in the book taken after 1965 show most engines in filthy condition, even if they were at the head of expresses. The days of employing engine cleaners had long gone. However, I was introduced by fellow photographer Paul Riley to the idea of restoring some pride to the last steam engines on BR before they were scrapped. The unofficial activity of getting some oil, paraffin and rags and cleaning up engines before later photographing them was a special time and, as this book will show, no one seemed to mind. A chapter recalls work on engines that operated from Holbeck (Leeds) and Carlisle (Kingmoor) in 1967. This closeness to the engines led to many joining railway and steam locomotive preservation societies, and I was no exception.

It is hard to believe that more than 50 years ago the first privately owned steam engine operated over the Settle & Carlisle line, on 1 April 1967. This often forgotten, fascinating period of steam preservation history is recalled as hundreds of BR steam

The first engine I cleaned was nothing less than a Gresley 'A4' 'Pacific' in July 1965. Here No 60027 *Merlin* is captured on Perth shed as myself (left), Dave Hartas and Paul Riley clean up the filthy loco, which we would later photograph on a passenger train to Edinburgh.

engines were in everyday operation at the same time. Four preserved main-line engines – *Clun Castle*, *Bittern*, *Flying Scotsman* and *Sir Nigel Gresley* – had traversed the line long before the '15 Guinea Special' of 11 August 1968.

However, BR had put in place a national steam ban preventing preserved engines from operating on its network from December 1967, and no one knew what the future held. It was a worrying time for loco owners, as the boiler life ticked away. Like many enthusiasts I had joined a preservation society – my local North Eastern Locomotive Preservation Group – and was deeply involved in saving the last surviving NER 'J27' and 'Q6' from going for scrap. I later became the group's Chief Mechanical Engineer, and working with some of the finest volunteers we returned three engines to main-line working that operated over the S&C. These included LNER Class 'K1' No 2005, Class 5 No 44767 *George Stephenson*, and one of Britain's most powerful locomotives, Peppercorn 'A2' 'Pacific' No 60532 *Blue Peter*. I was therefore able to work with some of the best BR footplate crews as I travelled on the footplate over the S&C and, with all my earlier photographic adventures, I knew just about every blade of grass along the route!

Having seen this special railway from both the lineside and the footplate of engines that I had helped to restore, it felt right to call the book *A Passion for Steam on the Settle & Carlisle Line*. I hope all readers will enjoy this journey through time, in which I have tried to capture the Settle & Carlisle Railway and steam in all their moods and reflect how lucky we are today to have steam operation 50 years after we thought it was the end.

Maurice Burns
July, 2018

1. In the beginning...

A first visit to the Settle & Carlisle Railway is often memorable for many different reasons. Mine was no exception, especially so as I was just 14 years old and I reached the line at Kirkby Stephen West after a 50-mile cycle ride from home. My confidence that such a ride was possible arose from the fact that I had just completed a week's cycle ride, with friend Chris Smith, to Edinburgh and on to Thornton shed, where Chris's father had once been shedmaster. That had been in April 1960 and steam was still plentiful; the highlight was seeing Gresley 'D49' 4-4-0 No 62733 *Northumberland* still in service.

Only days after that trip I decided I would go over the Pennines to Kirkby Stephen West station to see, among other things, the 'Royal Scots' on the 'Thames-Clyde' and 'Waverley' expresses. With just a Brownie camera, sandwiches and bottles of orange drink, I set off from Stockton-on-Tees on 25 April 1960.

At that time, passenger services over Stainmore from Darlington to Appleby and Penrith were still in operation using DMUs, and Kirkby Stephen loco shed (12D) was still in operation for freight traffic. The rail closures under the 'Beeching axe' were years away, and because of that I was still focused on reaching Kirkby Stephen West, the current station in operation on the S&C, rather than the Stainmore route.

For April it was a lovely day, with lots of sunshine but a head wind, and after I had passed through Barnard Castle I climbed to Stainmore summit and called at Barras station before descending to Kirkby Stephen. Climbing up the hill I passed over the East station and the loco shed right next to the road, where many locos were in steam. I reached the West station, which I had never been to before, just before lunchtime. It was so quiet and I had a look around and particularly liked the oil lamps, their shape so different from those on the North Eastern, and the huge station sign, the name so long that it needed two lines. With its Midland Railway signal box, a huge water tower and large goods shed, it was a typical country station. The silence was shattered by a heavy freight climbing up from Smardale hauled by a Hughes 'Crab' No 42881 going south, and 'Royal Scots' coming downhill on the 'Thames-Clyde' and 'Waverley'.

Below: The station oil lamps at Kirkby Stephen West were so different from those back home in the North East, and were duly photographed on 23 April 1960.

Above: After the 50-mile ride to Kirkby Stephen West I captured 'Crab' No 42881 heading a southbound freight on 23 April 1960; note my Jack Taylor bike leaning against the wall.

Right: The huge station sign at Kirkby Stephen West together with the Midland signal box can be seen as a 'Royal Scot' descends with 'The Thames-Clyde Express' on the same day.

Later in the afternoon I descended to Kirkby Stephen East station and walked round the shed, which was full of locomotives. Several were in steam, including No 78019, and soon another Standard 2MT, No 78017, arrived, was turned on the turntable and put on shed. It was late on a Saturday afternoon and the whole shed was so very quiet and still.

After a few shed pictures, which are now treasured, I set off on the 50-mile journey home via Brough, Barnard Castle and Darlington. Having just cycled through Brough and looking to the climb ahead, I noticed a trail of steam in the south leaving Kirkby Stephen. It was my natural instinct to race the engine to Stainmore summit, which still had an operational signal box, and that is what I did. I followed the trail of steam as it crossed Belah Viaduct, and when it got closer I found that it was Standard 4MT No 76049 travelling light engine back to West Auckland. Surprisingly we both reached the summit at the same time! The loco then took water while I raced on to Barnard Castle. I never knew who reached there first. When I got home I wrote up my log of my cycle ride, and it says, 'I was blown home by the wind.' It was a good day in every way!

Right: Returning home from Kirkby Stephen West, I called in at Kirkby Stephen shed on the North Eastern line. Here Ivatt 2-6-0 No 43009 and Standard 2-6-0 No 78019 were in steam on shed. Remarkably I would see No 78019 again, subsequently preserved, at Kirkby Stephen on 27 August 2011 (see page 93).

Below: My last picture at Kirkby Stephen shed captured Standard 2-6-0 No 78017 as it arrived on shed from shunting duties.

2. A day at Ais Gill signal box

My first visit to Ais Gill summit and its signal box was in March 1963, a fine sunny day, and I reached it by cycling up Wensleydale. I had earlier been given a book written by O. S. Nock and Eric Treacy called *Main Lines Across the Border*, and one of Eric Treacy's photographic classics was of immaculate 'Jubilee' No 45573 *Newfoundland* hauling 'The Waverley' nearing Ais Gill summit with Wild Boar Fell as a backdrop. It looked stunning, but first I had to study maps and contours to see where it was actually located.

Cycling up from the Moorcock Inn with Wild Boar Fell getting ever closer, I came to the summit bridge just as a stopping train

On a warm spring day in April 1964 LMS 8F 2-8-0 No 48038 makes a fine exhaust as it tops Ais Gill summit with the southbound Long Meg minerals.

was passing hauled by a Class 5. There were two paths to the signal box, one direct from the road through a gate and another on a path from under the summit bridge. As it was so quiet, I decided to walk to the box, climb the steps, knock on the door and ask the signalman if there was anything due. He made me feel welcome, so much so that I stayed there the whole day! He had the coal fire lit for keeping warm and making the tea – it was quite a cosy little signal box.

He got the bells from Garsdale or Kirkby Stephen and I would walk down the track to find a location for a picture, or take one from the box itself. In those days in the countryside, walking down the line or crossing the tracks at a lonely signal box was normal and I did not think anything of it. The signalman said nothing, it was a carefree age, and I never thought to ask, as it was what photographers did, and he understood what I was trying to do – capture BR steam before it was gone.

On this occasion I had borrowed my father's camera, a British-built metal-bodied Ilford Advocate, which had a fixed 35mm wide-angle lens with a maximum shutter speed of 1/200th of a second. He bought this camera for wide-angle views when rock-climbing in Glen Coe and Skye, but for me, while not quite ideal with a fixed 35mm lens, it was a step up from the Brownie!

Included here are a few images from that very pleasant Saturday afternoon shared with the signalman at Ais Gill signal box before I cycled the 50 miles to home. Without doubt, the southbound climb at Ais Gill summit with Wild Boar Fell as a backdrop must be one of the most spectacular locations in Britain to witness steam in action and, like many enthusiasts, I have been back, again and again…

A very enjoyable day was spent in Ais Gill box thanks to the signalman. Here is a view of the lever frame with the summit sign in the distance.

Viewed while standing between the tracks, LMS 8F 2-8-0 No 48318 speeds past the summit box with the northbound Long Meg empties.

Viewed from Ais Gill signal box, LMS 8F 2-8-0 No 48689 brings a load of vans northbound for Carlisle.

3. A hard day's night

As the sound of the Beatles and their hit record *A Hard Day's Night* in 1964 made the charts I made one of my own bravest records in terms of endurance. The dates of 27 and 28 November 1964 will be ones I will always recall with a sense of excitement for what I hoped would happen as I set off on my cycle into the darkness over Stainmore high in the Pennines. The trip was typical of the time when the rapid decline of steam and line closures under the 'Beeching axe' meant that you really wanted to be in two or three places on the same day. This was the case in this amazing period of just over 24 hours.

In January 1962 my local branch line from Darlington over Stainmore to Penrith had been closed beyond Barnard Castle, leaving the branch from there to Middleton-in-Teesdale open. Saturday 28 November 1964 was the day when the remaining line from Darlington to Middleton-in-Teesdale was to close. On the same day the Warwickshire Railway Society was running its 'Carlisle Railtour' with planned motive power of a 'Britannia' over Shap and one of the last 'Royal Scots' over the S&C. So while some of the accompanying pictures are not on the Settle & Carlisle, what I did before and after taking my railtour picture of 'Royal Scot' 4-6-0 No 46160 *Queen Victoria's Rifleman* on Smardale curve may be of interest.

After finishing work at 4.00pm I took my Jack Taylor bike, which was already loaded with cameras, flash gun, tripod, tape recorder, sleeping bag and supplies, on DMUs from Thornaby to Barnard Castle, travelling on the last ever Friday train and arriving at 6.07pm. This gave me a helping hand by almost halving the 65-mile cycle ride over Stainmore to Tebay, where I intended to spend the night to be ready for the railtour on the Saturday morning.

Although it was dark when I left Barnard Castle station, the weather was kind for November. There was a little wind from the west and a clear sky, but nearly freezing temperatures! After climbing over Stainmore, I dropped down into Kirkby Stephen where I bought some fish and chips, then climbed the hill to Kirkby Stephen West station where I ate them sat on a platform seat as night freights passed through. After having tea with the signalman sitting by his fire and seeing another 8F pass on its way to Ais Gill, it was back on the bike in the darkness and over the hill for the last 15 miles to Tebay. I arrived there just before midnight.

This was my first visit to Tebay shed and it will never be forgotten, with the noise of exhausts and whistling in the darkness throughout the night. There was just so much traffic at that time, either speeding south downhill or northbound freight trains stopping for a banker then restarting their heavy trains with a banker at the rear. There were two banking engines on duty, that night, Fairburn tanks Nos 42210 and 42110, which were sitting outside the shed bothy ready for action. Using tripod and flash gun, the banking engines and crew were captured in the darkness. Inside the bothy the enginemen made me welcome. We sat round the coal fire drinking tea hearing a freight slowly plod through the station to the foot of the bank, then whistle for a banker. The driver and fireman went outside, climbed aboard No 42210, moved her off the shed and eased up to the guard's van at the rear of the freight. Following the exchange of whistles the train disappeared noisily up the bank and into the darkness. Just how the people in Tebay ever slept I will never know!

Scout Green box we were soon passing the distant lights of Shap Wells Hotel and into the steep-sided summit cutting. As we approached the Summit signal box the driver of No 42110 slammed shut the regulator

After three rides on the Shap bankers to the summit, a brief moment of quiet sees Fairburn 2-6-4 tanks Nos 42210 and 42110 standing outside Tebay shed bothy awaiting their next call of duty. This picture was taken at 1.00am on 28 November 1964.

Moments later another freight hauled by one of the last 'Patriots', No 45531 *Sir Frederick Harrison*, whistled for assistance and the driver of banker No 42110 offered me a trip to the summit. After the buffers of the tank engine touched the guard's van and the distinctive 'crow' whistles were exchanged, it was soon full regulator for the banker engine. There was so much exhaust noise, and much shovelling of coal into the firebox by the poor fireman. Looking forward into the darkness at the 'Patriot' at the front of the freight, it could not be heard at all. Indeed, we joked that it was taking it easy and leaving all the work to the banker! After and slowly the guard's van tail light moved away as if by magic. Once the banker was stationary we could hear the distant exhaust of the 'Patriot' at the front end of the freight. A quick descent of the bank followed, where a Class 5 with a freight was waiting for assistance. I made two more trips to the summit, but as 3.00am approached it was time for a sleep.

I was hoping to find somewhere warm to sleep in the shed buildings, but the facilities were non-existent. The shed had been constructed in 1861 and modernised in 1947, but the office looked to be original and was no more than a bothy in which to make a cup of tea. In desperation to get my head down, the floor of a guard's van became my bedroom. With lilo and sleeping bag I was warm enough, but only enjoyed interrupted sleep due to banking engines passing within feet and, of course, the whistling.

When I awoke the next morning I could not believe my eyes – it was snowing! Freight after freight arrived for a banker, then 'Jubilee' No 45563 *Australia* arrived in the station with the Warrington to Carlisle all-stations stopping train. The next arrival took me by surprise, as Class 5 No 44931 was towing dead 'Duchess' 'Pacific' No 46257 *City of Salford* to Arnott Young's scrapyard at Troon – the whole class had been withdrawn en bloc six weeks earlier.

By mid-morning the sky had totally cleared as I cycled through Orton up to Shap Wells, where I caught several Class 5s, a 'Clan' 'Pacific' and freights or parcel trains all banked by the Fairburn tanks. The lighting conditions were perfect with a combination of snow, sun and steam! I had made this trip to see the Warwickshire Railway Society railtour hauled by a 'Britannia'. However, it was not to be. The rostered 'Britannia' failed on shed, to be replaced by No 70052 *Firth of Tay*. This 'Britannia' then failed with injector problems near Carnforth, and was itself replaced by Class 5 No 45018, which gave a magnificent performance climbing Shap, most appreciated by the enthusiasts on board looking out of the carriage windows the length of the train. While the lack of a 'Britannia' was disappointing, the picture of No 45018 in such brilliant weather conditions was special, well worth all the cycling!

I then cycled back to Smardale Viaduct

After overnight snow and a cycle ride from Tebay to Shap Wells, I captured Class 5 No 45018, deputising for a failed 'Britannia', climbing the Shap gradient in fine style with the Warwickshire Railway Society's 'Carlisle Railtour' on 28 November 1964.

just north of Kirkby Stephen, where I climbed up to the line from the stream to see Standard Class 4 2-6-0 No 76084 emerge from Crosby Garrett Tunnel on a southbound freight (this engine was subsequently preserved). A Class 5 then crossed the viaduct before the Warwickshire Railway Society special came into view round Smardale curve hauled by 'Royal Scot' 4-6-0 No 46160 *Queen Victoria's Rifleman*.

Because of the loco failures, the special was running late over the S&C, and I

Prior to seeing the railtour return over the S&C, I caught Standard 4 2-6-0 No 76084 emerging from Crosby Garrett Tunnel with a southbound freight.

Not long after No 76084 had passed, a unidentified Class 5 crossed Smardale Viaduct with a southbound train of vans.

In fading light the Warwickshire Railway Society special came into view round Smardale curve hauled by 'Royal Scot' 4-6-0 No 46160 *Queen Victoria's Rifleman*.

was getting worried. I still had to cycle to Barnard Castle station to catch the 6.09pm train – not any train, but the last train – to Middleton-in-Teesdale. In fading light I climbed towards Brough and on to Stainmore. It was now dark. Once over the top with a tail wind and going downhill I was speeding along, and after Bowes descended into Barnard Castle. As I crossed the River Tees I looked at my watch – I had less than 10 minutes to climb the hill to reach the station to see the last train arrive. With much relief I made it. Now with my bike on the train, I was with hundreds of enthusiasts for the last train to Middleton-in-Teesdale, then back to Darlington, which was duly photographed with a flash. When I told my friends on the train of my 'hard day's night', which had included riding on the footplate of the Shap bankers, they did not believe me, but it was all true. It was a truly an incredible 24 hours!

After cycling over Stainmore to catch the last train from Barnard Castle to Middleton-in-Teesdale, I travelled on the 7.00pm Middleton-in-Teesdale to Darlington DMU – the last passenger train before the line was closed. Here at 7.20pm a flash picture captures the last moments at Barnard Castle before the train departed for Darlington on 28 November 1964.

4. Garsdale to Keighley explorer

It is true to say that the Settle & Carlisle line is at its finest when the sun shines, but when it rains, as it regularly does, it is at its most atmospheric! At Easter 1965 I planned to explore the line south from Garsdale for the first time, staying at Youth Hostels on the way, but that weekend the weather was really dreadful with rain and drizzle for three days. On Good Friday I cycled up Wensleydale to Garsdale, getting drenched on the way, but saw a 'WD' on freight and the steam-hauled stopping train near Moorcock Tunnel. I had a look at Garsdale station, which still had a water tower and two water columns for southbound trains, but the track had just been removed from Platform 3. The hard climb over the Coal Road to Dent station followed, then I turned left up the valley to Dent Youth Hostel, where I planned to stay – but when I went to book in I found it was full.

'No bother,' said the warden. 'There's a

After a wet cycle ride through Wensleydale from home, the rain eased as LMS Class 5 No 45210 departed from Garsdale with a Hellifield to Carlisle stopping train. The second coach looks to be non-corridor stock.

Emerging from Moorcock Tunnel is 'WD' 2-8-0 No 90518 on a southbound mixed freight from Carlisle Kingmoor.

cottage just down the road – turn first right past some houses near the viaduct and make yourself at home.'

The cottage was next to Arten Gill Viaduct and while the wood fire dried out my clothes and steam trains ran almost above our head, I was, by a twist of fate, in paradise!

Next morning the weather was little better with a fine drizzle, but after seeing freights cross Arten Gill Viaduct I cycled up the valley to Dent Head. Just as I was approaching Dent Head Viaduct I heard the sound of a train coming out of Blea Moor Tunnel – a very short train with a 4F hauling just one wagon of coal for Dent station. It soon dropped this off and in minutes was heading south for Skipton as engine and van.

As I climbed up to the lineside a 'WD' headed south, and I then walked to the

Viewed from the cottage provided by Dent Youth Hostel, a southbound freight hauled by a Class 5 crosses Arten Gill Viaduct early on that misty wet morning.

When cycling up Dentdale and approaching Dent Head Viaduct a rumble in Blea Moor Tunnel gave warning of an oncoming train. What emerged was unexpected – a 4F with one wagon of coal for Dent station.

entrance of Blea Moor Tunnel. I did not have to wait long before a rumble inside the tunnel indicated that a train was on its way. I was fully expecting a Class 5, but out came one of the last working 'Royal Scots', No 46128 *The Lovat Scouts* on a northbound freight. This one picture made the whole weekend worthwhile.

Back on the bike, wearing my cycle cape to try and keep dry, I saw Ribblehead

The easterly wind plays havoc with the exhaust of an unidentified 'WD' on a southbound freight. From this unusual position, the picture illustrates the height of Dent Head Viaduct.

A walk to Blea Moor Tunnel to photograph whatever next came out turned out to be my favourite picture of the weekend. Ex-LMS 'Royal Scot' No 46128 *The Lovat Scouts* makes a fine sight as it emerges from the tunnel with a northbound freight for Carlisle.

Viaduct for the first time and, after visiting Ribblehead station, which was very run down, saw an 8F storm through. Continuing down the valley calling at Horton-in-Ribblesdale and Settle stations, I managed to get a picture of 'Jubilee' No 45660 *Rooke* approaching Settle at speed with an excursion to Glasgow. It appeared without warning as I had no knowledge of what was due.

Upon reaching Hellifield I had a look at the station and the closed loco shed, where I was told unrestored steam

The wet weather continued, and so did the picture-taking. Here a filthy ex-LMS 8F, with its smokebox number plate unrecognisable, powers through Ribblehead station, with the station master's house on the left of the picture.

Just south of Settle, where the road goes under the line, the unexpected roar of a 'Jubilee' was heard. No 45660 *Rooke* charges the 'Long Drag' with a Leeds to Glasgow excursion.

engines for the National Collection were stored. Another enthusiast told me it was possible to go inside the locked shed by a secret entrance at the rear of the building – so I had to have a look. Inside was Hughes/ Fowler 'Crab' No 42700 and a loco close to my heart – North Eastern Railway Class 'Q7' 0-8-0 No 63460, which in my later life I was responsible for restoring to working order. Back at the station I managed to get a picture of 'Britannia' No 70039 *Sir Christopher Wren* departing for the south on an excursion, but the image of the steam leaks and the rain summed up the day.

Despite my best efforts I was soaked, so decided that, as I planned to stay in the Burley-in-Wharfedale Youth Hostel that night, I would catch a train from Hellifield

At Hellifield a fellow enthusiast showed me the way to see the National Railway Museum's reserve collection. Inside the shed the North Eastern Railway's most powerful 0-8-0, Class 'Q7' No 63460, shares company with LMS 'Crab' No 42700.

In pouring rain BR Standard 'Britannia' No 70039 *Sir Christopher Wren*, in poor mechanical condition judging by the front-end steam leaks, departs from Hellifield with a Leeds City passenger train.

to Keighley to get me there in a reasonable time. The next train was from Morecambe, and arrived hauled by 'Jubilee' No 45592 *Indore*. On the journey I passed three steam-hauled freights as well as Skipton steam shed with a 'Jinty' as shed pilot. Alighting at Keighley's wet platform with my bike, I cycled to the Burley-in-Wharfedale hostel for much-needed warmth and hot food.

While the weather was certainly not good for this trip, I had now explored for the first time the line south from Garsdale and knew, in some detail, the remoteness of the line with its incredible huge viaducts and tunnels. I would be back again and again....

Now soaked through, I decided to catch the next train from Hellifield to Keighley. Ex-LMS 'Jubilee' No 45592 *Indore* is seen arriving, with the coaling plant for the closed shed on the right.

Approaching Skipton, this view from the train captures the shed scene and Skipton Engine Shed signal box with a 'Jinty' shunting the sidings.

The wet platforms of Keighley station are clearly visible as 'Jubilee' No 45592 *Indore* departs for Leeds City. The preserved Keighley & Worth Valley Railway was already in existence at this time, the Worth Valley branch being behind the 'Jubilee'.

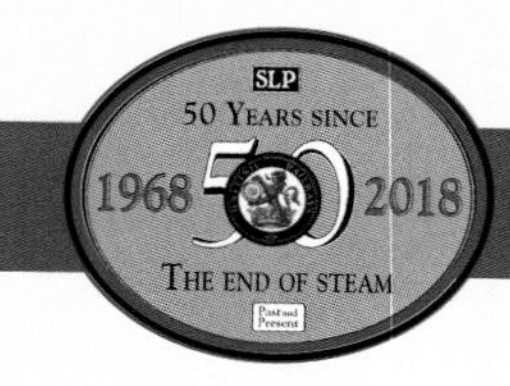

5. Memories of Carlisle Kingmoor

My first visit to Carlisle Kingmoor shed, coded 12A, was when I was about 12 years old. Carlisle had four locomotive sheds at that time, and all were visited. Durran Hill closed on 2 November 1959, then Canal on 17 June 1963 and Upperby on 12 December 1966, leaving Kingmoor the last steam shed in the Border City. After Canal closed Carlisle had no LNER allocations. However, Edinburgh St Margaret's shed's allocation of 'B1s', 'V2s' and 'A3s' still traversed the Waverley route, so in 1965, if you were lucky, you could see a 'V2' or one of the last three remaining 'A3s', Nos 60041 *Salmon Trout*, 60052 *Prince Palatine* and 60100 *Spearmint*.

Up to 1964 'Duchesses' could be seen on Kingmoor and I well remember seeing Nos 46455 *City of Hereford* and 46457 *City of Salford* with 12A shedplates. However, none of the LNER engines or 'Duchesses' were diagrammed for the S&C. The other classes of engine in 1964 and 1965 that were always looked for were 'Patriots' and 'Royal Scots'. The remaining members of both classes were at Kingmoor and they would work any route, including the S&C. During the period of steam's declining years it was always the unusual locos you would look out for, and if Nos 45512, 45531, 46115, 46128, 46140 or 46160 were spotted on shed you would go to the roster board to find their next working.

Kingmoor was a massive shed with a huge allocation of up to 150 locomotives, but it frequently had transfers from other shed engines that had no work for them. The best examples of this were the 'Britannia' 'Pacifics', where 40 or the class of 55 were at Kingmoor to work out their final days. For some, the work from Carlisle on freights was a far cry from the glamour of their days working the 'Golden Arrow', when working from London.

Besides the express engines there was a large allocation of ex-LMS Class 5s and 8Fs, 9Fs and even at one time Crosti-boilered 9Fs for freight traffic. Then there was a large allocation of Ivatt 4MTs with even the prototype, No 43000, which starred on the 'Wansbeck Piper' railtour, finding its way from Blyth to Kingmoor. The 4MTs worked on passenger services to Appleby and freights to Langholm on the Waverley route and Kirkby Stephen East on the old North Eastern line. No 43121 was also rostered for a railtour that was the last steam passenger train on the Alston branch.

Kingmoor had a large mechanical coaling plant and good workshop facilities, which may explain why it was the last shed in Carlisle. When visiting I would always look inside the workshop to see which engines were having piston and valve exams, and it gave a lift when one of the last four 'Royal Scots', No 46160 *Queen Victoria's Rifleman*, was being serviced for further work when 67 of its classmates had been withdrawn for scrap.

My last two visits to Kingmoor were for different reasons. On 14 October 1967 ex-GWR 'Castle' No 7029 *Clun Castle* had arrived in Carlisle via Shap on a railtour and was being serviced prior to working south over the S&C. Even though Kingmoor was to close in a few months, the shed was still full of Class 5s, 8Fs, 9Fs and 'Britannias'. It was a sobering thought that immaculate *Clun Castle*, its future secured in preservation, was surrounded by dozens of engines most of which had only one fate – the scrapyard.

Fortunately one of the Class 5s that was alongside No 7029, No 44767, did make it into preservation.

My very last visit was with friends to polish up No 70013 *Oliver Cromwell* on the evening of Christmas Day 1967, as it was to work a football excursion to Blackpool on Boxing Day. This was to be the last BR steam passenger train over Shap, and within five days Kingmoor, the last steam shed in Carlisle, was closed for good. But for any enthusiast who visited this huge shed full of engines, the memories will live on.

In the smoke-filled shed yard at Carlisle Kingmoor in July 1964 ex-LMS 'Duchess' No 46257 *City of Salford* is being prepared for duty. Allocated to Kingmoor for West Coast Main Line duties, this engine was one of two built in 1947 with roller bearings, and had a short working life of only 17 years.

Gresley 'V2' No 60955 backs down into Kingmoor shed after bringing a freight from Edinburgh over the Waverley route to Kingmoor yard in July 1964. Kingmoor saw many LNER locos following the closure of Canal shed.

Ex-LMS 'Jubilee' No 45626 *Seychelles* arrives at Kingmoor on a Saturday afternoon in August 1964, having earlier worked an express over the S&C.

Walking round Kingmoor and finding a Gresley 'A3' such as No 60100 *Spearmint* was like striking gold, as there were only three operational 'A3s' in April 1965 when this picture was taken – the rest had been scrapped. The engine later worked over the Waverley route on a freight to Edinburgh.

Ex-LMS 4Fs were regular visitors to Carlisle, though by late 1964 they were becoming rare. A Sunday morning shed visit finds No 44028 – the crew who brought the engine to Carlisle were obviously football fans.

By 1965, even though steam days were numbered, repairs to inspection pits continued. This picture captures three gems: a Gresley 'V2' on the left, 'Patriot' No 45531 *Sir Fredrick Harrison* in the distance, and on the right one of the last 'Royal Scots', No 46160 *Queen Victoria's Rifleman*.

Left: The BR Standard 'Clan' Class was only introduced in 1952, yet many were withdrawn after less than ten years in service. However, a batch at Kingmoor lived on and did useful work that included trains over the S&C. Here No 72006 *Clan Mackenzie*, recently overhauled, carries the name of its home shed on the buffer beam.

Below: Any visit to Kingmoor would always include a look into the repair shops. On this occasion there was good news as one of the last 'Royal Scots', No 46160 *Queen Victoria's Rifleman*, receives attention for further service.

trough water tank, almost pinching myself – was this really happening and did the train have any passengers? The train was perhaps a legacy of one that had started from Hawes in Midland Railway days. The service ceased operation within months of the picture being taken and No 84015, with other members of her class, was withdrawn from Skipton shed by the end of the year and went for scrap.

From Garsdale station we collected our bikes and bought some snacks at the shop that existed at that time, then cycled to Ais Gill summit, taking pictures of the many steam freights on the way at Moorcock

Shortly behind *Clan Macleod* was another unusual Standard in the form of rebuilt Crosti-boilered 9F No 92022 on a heavy southbound freight.

Cycling back to Garsdale, and shortly before going over the Coal Road, Class 5 No 45012 speeds through the station with a southbound passenger excursion, one of many seen on that July day.

Tunnel and other places. At around 9.40am at Ais Gill we photographed the southbound 8.05am Carlisle to Hellifield stopping passenger train hauled by BR Standard 'Clan' No 72008 *Clan Macleod*. This was followed minutes later by Crosti-boilered 9F 2-10-0 No 92022 on a southbound freight. Progressively, we cycled back to Garsdale where passenger excursions hauled by Class 5s passed through, one of which I caught on the troughs taking water.

The next part of the day's plan was to cycle over the hilly road known as the Coal Road from Garsdale to Dent station to take pictures at Dent for an hour, before catching No 72008 *Clan Macleod* on its return working to Carlisle as far as Garsdale. It seemed a good idea at the time! At Dent we saw 'Jubilee' 4-6-0 No 45573 *Newfoundland* and a Class 5 on passenger excursions heading north, and 9Fs on freights. At 12.57 *Clan Macleod* rolled into Dent from Hellifield and we loaded our bikes onto the train for the short journey through Rise Hill Tunnel past the hut at the troughs – our sleeping quarters – before arriving at Garsdale. Here we quickly unloaded our bikes and, sprinting up the track, were able to photograph No 72008 leaving for Carlisle.

It was only just after 1.00pm and the day

Above: Arriving at Dent and walking to Rise Hill Tunnel, we saw Class 5 No 44802 on a northbound passenger excursion to Glasgow, with Dentdale in the background.

Left: Back at Dent station, another Class 5, No 44671, speeds through with a southbound freight.

This is an interesting view of how Dent station looked in steam days with the signal box clearly in use. At 12.57pm BR Standard 'Clan' No 72008 *Clan Macleod* arrives with the Hellifield to Carlisle stopping train.

After the short journey through Rise Hill Tunnel behind the 'Clan', at Garsdale having unloaded our cycles, we saw No 72008 *Clan Macleod* as it departed from Garsdale.

A walk to Garsdale troughs saw Class 5 No 45295, viewed from the top of the water tank, taking water from the troughs as it headed a southbound excursion to Leeds.

had been brilliant so far, but more surprises were in store. We cycled back up to Ais Gill for the afternoon trains climbing to the summit. We were caught by surprise as 'Jubilee' 4-6-0 No 45697 *Achilles* descended from the summit on a northbound passenger excursion. Three more Class 5-hauled freights then a 9F on the southbound Long Meg minerals followed, but we knew that the southbound 'CTAC Scottish Tours Express', which was normally 'Jubilee'-hauled, was due, and headed for Ais Gill Viaduct. The train was hauled by No 45573 *Newfoundland*, the second time we had seen it that day; the fireman, with knotted white handkerchief on his head, produced a memorable exhaust. Not far behind the 'Jubilee' was BR Standard 'Britannia' No 70003 *John Bunyan* on the 4.37pm Carlisle to Bradford stopping train, which passed Ais Gill at 6.15pm.

In the evening sunshine we saw two 8F-hauled freights near Ais Gill box, the

We were caught by surprise by 'Jubilee' No 45697 *Achilles* as it topped the summit at Ais Gill with a northbound passenger train to Glasgow.

In the late afternoon filthy 'Jubilee' 4-6-0 No 45573 *Newfoundland* crosses Ais Gill Viaduct with the CTAC Gourock to Leicester train, laying on a lovely exhaust.

Back at Ais Gill summit for the afternoon trains, the first into view was Standard 9F No 92009 on the southbound Long Meg minerals.

The 4.37pm Carlisle to Bradford stopping train approaches Ais Gill summit hauled by BR Standard 'Britannia' No 70003 *John Bunyan.*

signalman keeping us informed of what was due. He then told us that there was another freight in section from Kirkby Stephen. Walking down the line, which was the norm in those days, we could see the freight near Mallerstang. I fully expected another Class 5, but as I looked in the distance it had the smoke deflectors of one of the last 'Patriots' or 'Royal Scots'. As the train of mineral empties came under the road bridge we could see that it was one of the last three 'Royal Scots' – No 46115 *Scots Guardsman.*

We then called it a day – all 16 hours of sunshine – and cycled to the Youth Hostel high up on the hillside at Shaws, Lunds, not far from Ais Gill summit. We both slept like logs and on Sunday morning cycled home to Stockton-on-Tees having had one of the best day's photography on the Settle & Carlisle line.

In the last hours of daylight on 17 July 1965, what was thought to be another Class 5 on a freight turned out to be one of the last 'Royal Scots', No 46115 *Scots Guardsman*, on a southbound minerals. The engine had earlier worked the 9.50am Edinburgh to Carlisle passenger train over the Waverley route. This final picture of the day was a fitting end to a great day with camera and cycle.

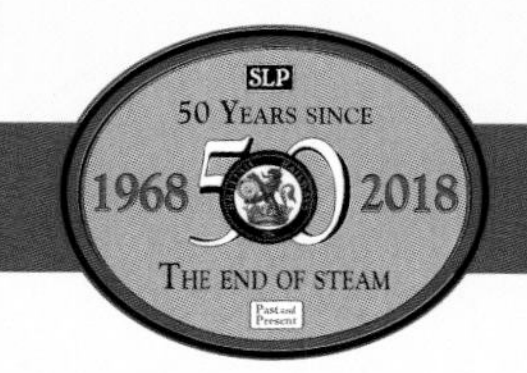

6. A busy day at Hellifield

Hellifield in its prime must have been a major junction, being a station of some distinction with four platforms and a large loco shed for an allocation of 40 engines. The loss of the passenger service from Hellifield to Clitheroe and Blackburn in 1962, which used the bay Platform 3 at the east, together with the general reduction in traffic, saw Hellifield loco shed closed from 17 June 1963 – the same date as Carlisle Canal shed. The shed was retained to house items from the National Collection for many years and the turntable was retained to turn engines from Carlisle, used on the morning stopping train.

Against this background, one would think the number of trains calling at Hellifield would be low, and generally that was so, but in a six-week period in the summer, with all the Saturday-only extras from and to Morecambe, Leeds, Bradford and Carlisle, it returned to being a very busy station with 34 trains stopping – but only that large number on Saturdays!

It was during this period that I called at Hellifield station and the summit of the line south of the station in August 1965 to watch what passed through. Luckily I was able to see Class 5 No 44767 in the northbound bay Platform 2 being used for the 12.08 Hellifield stopping train to Carlisle.

At that time steam was so plentiful it was hard to envisage that within two years it would be all gone and the bay Platform 3 would be used no more....

Viewed from the site of the closed Hellifield loco shed, seen on the right, 'Britannia' No 70009 *Alfred the Great* brings a Glasgow to Leeds excursion through Hellifield.

At the south end of Hellifield, with the junction to Blackburn to the left, 'Jubilee' No 45697 *Achilles* speeds through Hellifield with a Glasgow to Leeds excursion.

Seen from alongside Hellifield South Junction signal box, 8F No 48218 steams through the station with a southbound freight. The rails in the island platform have been disconnected and will see no further use.

8F No 48301 brings a heavy track panel train past Hellifield South Junction signal box bound for Ais Gill and beyond.

Not far from Hellifield is the summit of the line to Bell Busk and Skipton. Here two Class 5s are about to cross, with No 45209 nearest the camera on a Morecambe train.

Above: At the summit of the line south of Hellifield, this picture sums up the state of steam locomotives in 1965. The fireman of truly filthy 'Jubilee' No 45660 *Rooke* prepares the fire for the climb beyond Hellifield to Carlisle with a relief 'Thames-Clyde Express'.

Right: Class 5 No 44778 brings a Morecambe to Bradford stopping train into Hellifield, passing Standard 9F No 92110 on the Long Meg mineral empties. The closed Hellifield shed, used to store engines destined for the National Collection, is in the background.

In this busy scene at Hellifield, a Class 5 with empty stock stands on the right, Standard 9F No 92110 is on the southbound Long Meg minerals, and 'Jubilee' No 45626 *Seychelles* speeds through the station with a excursion from Leeds to Glasgow.

The Hellifield north bay platform was still in use in 1965 for the Hellifield to Carlisle stopping train. Here Class 5 No 44767, fitted with outside Stephenson valve gear, waits for a handful of passengers before departure.

8. A SUMMER SATURDAY AT LEEDS CITY STATION

In the summer of 1965 I was aware of the intensive steam operation on the Settle & Carlisle line, with up to ten passenger excursions per Saturday, and even the stopping trains steam-hauled. This was a far cry from the North East where I lived, where the East Coast Main Line had no regular steam haulage. In the North East there were still a handful of Peppercorn 'A1s' about, mainly on standby duties in case of diesel failures. Leeds Neville Hill shed did have a number of 'A1s', and when the 1965 timetable was published there was a summer Saturday-only Leeds to Newcastle express that was 'A1'-hauled for the six weeks of operation, and it was routed via Harrogate and Ripon rather than York.

I therefore decided to visit Leeds City station and photograph the steam departures. I had a bonus in that a Fowler tank, No 42410, was on station pilot duties that day. Here are some images captured on that enjoyable day, which included two 'Jubilees', Nos 45647 and 45593, and Peppercorn 'A1' 'Pacific' No 60131 *Osprey*, all heading westward within a few hours. Happy days!

It was a real bonus on the visit to Leeds City station in August 1965 to see 'Jubilees' and a Peppercorn 'Pacific', to also find an LMS Fowler tank on station pilot duties. Here No 42410 departs from the station with empty stock.

'Jubilee' No 45697 *Achilles* lays on a magnificent exhaust as it departs from Leeds City with an excursion to Glasgow, while a Class 5 awaits departure at an adjoining platform.

Taken moments later, this interesting picture shows No 42410 bringing empty stock into Leeds City station, while a 'Peak' diesel and 'Jubilee' No 45593 *Kolhapur* await departure for the Settle & Carlisle.

'Jubilee' No 45593 *Kolhapur* departs for the Settle & Carlisle on the relief 'Thames-Clyde Express'.

A handful of remaining Peppercorn Class 'A1' 'Pacifics' were allocated to Leeds Neville Hill shed for work mainly to York or Newcastle via Harrogate or when Holbeck was short of motive power over the Settle & Carlisle line. On this occasion No 60131 *Osprey* departs from Leeds City with the 13.37 summer-only Leeds to Newcastle passenger train via Harrogate and Ripon.

9. Day return to Settle

During November 1965 there was heavy snow on the Pennines and news reports of blocked roads with snow ploughs in action on the railways. The main route from the North East to the S&C was via the A66 over Stainmore, which was blocked by drifts. Against this uncertain background, together with friend John Emmerson I explored the possibilities of seeing the S&C steam-hauled stopping train near Settle by travelling by train from Stockton-on-Tees.

With such a poor service of only two stopping trains in each direction on the S&C, we imagined it would be impossible to arrive there by train and get a picture. However, a Glasgow express from Leeds made a stop at Settle just under an hour ahead of the steam-hauled stopping train from Hellifield to Carlisle. So we could do it. The aim was to get a picture high above Settle of the train departing for Carlisle. It was a long way to go for one picture. I had never explored the Settle photographic location before and it was chosen by examining a map. A lot of walking in heavy snow would be involved. There was also the small problem of getting home from Settle. There was the southbound 'Thames-Clyde Express' at 12.56, but the chances of getting that after taking the photo from up on the hillside were remote.

Viewed from the train travelling from Leeds to Settle, the pulse quickened as we passed Skipton shed where two Standard Class 4s, No 75057 and 75058, coupled between two snow ploughs, were being coaled ready for use on the S&C.

The alternative northbound 'Thames-Clyde' called at 15.37, but that would mean a long journey back via Carlisle, and later still the next southbound stopping train was not until 18.54! Amazingly, Settle had, and in effect still has, two stations, the other being Giggleswick, and we saw that it was possible to return from Giggleswick via Leeds. Having done our considerable homework and now confident that we could get there and back, we bought our day return tickets from Thornaby to Settle for a brilliant day with many surprises.

With a 07.34 start from Thornaby,

Above: Upon arrival at Settle we climbed to a high viewpoint where the camera caught Standard 4s Nos 75057 and 75058 on snow-clearing duties. Unbeknown to me at the time, this picture also captured other snow-clearing duties as men clear the white lines on a football pitch!

changing at Darlington and York, we took the first steam pictures of the day passing York, capturing Nos 65823 and 77000. At Leeds we boarded the 10.25 for Carlisle and Glasgow. Passing Skipton loco shed we saw two large snow ploughs at either end of two Standard Class 4s, Nos 75057 and 75058, which were being coaled and made ready to clear snowdrifts on the S&C.

Arriving at Settle at 11.28 we quickly walked through the town and up the snowclad hillside to get into position before the stopping train from Hellifield to Carlisle departed at 12.20. No sooner had we found our elevated position than the two plough engines passed through heading north at the same time as a mineral train descended. Then the steam-hauled stopping train hauled by Class 5 No 44675 was photographed crossing the viaduct north of Settle heading for Carlisle. We had accomplished our mission, and had also seen four steam-hauled trains in an hour, but we had to get home.

With about an hour to catch our train or face a very late arrival back home, we quickly walked through Settle to Giggleswick station. It was just less than 3 miles away, but we did the walk on the snow-covered roads in good time. We were surprised to find LNER Class 'B1' 4-6-0 No 61309 on the train as it rolled into Giggleswick – 'B1' haulage had never been on the day's agenda! After passing through Hellifield we decided, at the last minute, to get off at Gargrave

Above: The main purpose of the day return to Settle was to see the Hellifield to Carlisle stopping train depart from Settle. Here Class 5 No 44675 is seen shortly after leaving the station heading through the snow-covered landscape.

Left: After a walk from Settle to Giggleswick we caught the train to Leeds, though when we found the motive power was a 'B1' we decided to go only as far as Gargrave. 'B1' No 61309 is seen arriving at Giggleswick, which judging by the wagons on the right still had a good trade in coal traffic.

to take a picture of the 'B1' departing. A consequence of this hasty decision was that we then had to walk the 5 miles along snow-covered roads to Skipton. Another surprise awaited us there when Class 5 No 45156 *Ayrshire Yeomanry* was joined after a few minutes by another Class 5, No 44662, with both engines heading north on parcel trains to Morecambe and Colne. With flash and time exposures of the Class 5's in the bag, we were on trains again to Leeds and York, arriving home after 9.30pm.

It had been a long day but the sun shone on the snow-covered landscape from dawn to dusk. We had walked for miles, but the meticulous study of the map and railway timetables and careful planning had paid off, with mission accomplished!

Alighting at Gargrave station, we walked quickly down the line to see the 'B1' No 61309 make a high exhaust as it departed. A 5-mile walk along snow-covered roads was then the only way to catch a train home from Skipton.

Above: Upon arrival at Skipton station from Gargrave we found Class 5 No 45156 *Ayreshire Yeomanry* on a Morcambe parcels. Within a few minutes another Class 5, No 44662, arrived on another parcels train for Colne and was duly photographed before we caught our train home after an excellent day's photography.

10. The 'Lakes & Fells Rail Tour'

In early 1966 the Stephenson Locomotive Society and the Manchester Locomotive Society, which had run many joint railtours in the past, announced one for 2 April 1966 called the 'Lakes & Fells Rail Tour'. The name alone was enough to get my pulse racing and the route was no disappointment as it traversed the Settle & Carlisle and Lake District lines.

What made this tour a 'must see' was that, in addition to 'Jubilee' haulage by No 45596 *Bahamas* from Manchester Victoria to Hellifield, then Alan Pegler's 'A3' 'Pacific' No 4472 *Flying Scotsman* from Hellifield over the S&C to Carlisle and Penrith, it would be the last ever steam-hauled train from Penrith through Keswick to Workington, just two weeks before the line from Keswick to Workington was to close for good. The steam haulage and the lines traversed were amazing enough, but then nature added another dimension – snow!

Normally I would have aimed to see *Flying Scotsman* on the S&C, then travel over to the Keswick line to see the last steam train. However, as the day approached the weather deteriorated and snow ploughs were in action trying to keep the roads clear across the Pennines. Twenty-four hours before the trip, Manchester had 15 inches of snow, all public transport was at a standstill, and Glasgow to London trains were running 2 hours late. On the railways snow ploughs were in action with steam power, and roads from the North East to the Lakes, such as the A66, were blocked with ploughs trying to reopen them.

My friend John Emmerson and I both

Skipton shed's big ploughs at either end of Standard Class 4 Nos 75015 and 75057 had cleared the Settle & Carlisle line ahead of the 'Lakes & Fells Rail Tour' and are seen here taking water at Garsdale on 2 April 1966. *John Boyes, ARPT*

Gresley 'A3' 'Pacific' No 4472 *Flying Scotsman* speeds the railtour through snow-covered Garsdale. *John Boyes, ARPT*

wanted to see this trip, but we decided to go separately because of the roads being blocked by snow. John decided to try and reach Garsdale to see *Flying Scotsman* even though he had no knowledge of how bad the roads were. Because the weather forecast was not good, it was with much trepidation that John's father loaned him the family Cortina. Picking up two friends, he left Eaglescliffe for Northallerton, then headed up Wensleydale. The road and weather got worse approaching Hawes.

There were not many other cars on the road and, unlike today, when Hawes is busy all the year, it was like a ghost town, so John sought advice on road conditions at the Police House, but the policeman was out. Reassurance that the road was OK came from photographer John Boyes, who was also aiming to photograph No 4472. He had already been some distance down the road to Garsdale, and why he had turned back we will never know. Maybe he was glad to see John, as four can get a car out of a snowdrift more easily than one! Apart from a minor incident with drifting snow on the road, Garsdale was reached and the special was photographed speeding through, as well as two Standard Class 4s, Nos 75015 and 75057, coupled back-to-back with a large snow plough on each end, and the northbound stopping train leaving Garsdale.

An attempt to get to Ais Gill Summit was made, but the road was blocked with snow, a plough being dug out of the drift by its crew. It seemed that on that day at least, the BR advert 'Fog and snow the trains still go' was true!

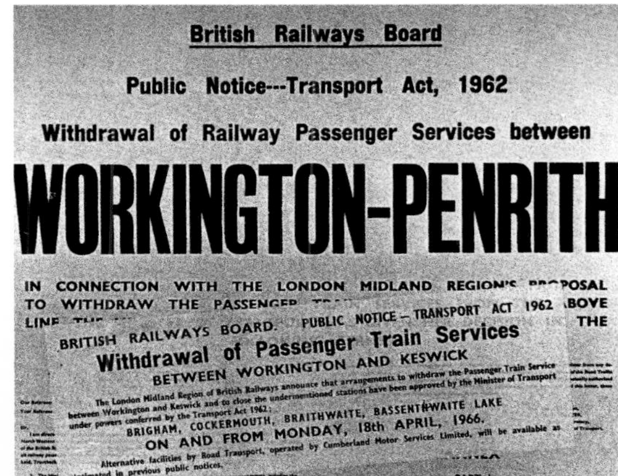

Above right: On 2 April 1966 the Penrith to Keswick DMU descends from Troutbeck through the snow-covered landscape with the high peak of Saddleback in the distance.

Right: The line closure notice at Keswick station.

Left: A poster for cheap day return fares from Keswick. Services to Cockermouth and Workington were withdrawn 14 days after the picture was taken.

Right: In a beautiful location, the 'Lakes & Fells Rail Tour' skirts Bassenthwaite Lake hauled by Ivatt 2-6-0s Nos 46458 and 46426, with the snow-capped peak of Skiddaw in the distance. This was the last steam train over this line before closure two weeks later.

The Cortina was returned safe and sound, much to the relief of John's father.

My day was somewhat different. I decided to put all my eggs in one basket and make the long rail journey by train from Darlington via Newcastle, Carlisle and Penrith, then down the line to Keswick and on to Bassenthwaite Lake station – a long way for just one picture of the 'Lakes & Fells Rail Tour'. However, it was an incredible day with the snow-capped mountains of Saddleback and Skiddaw viewed from my only ever journey on the Keswick line. I also photographed some of the last passenger trains between Keswick and Workington in brilliant weather conditions, under a clear blue sky against a backdrop of snow-capped mountains.

Near the beautiful Bassenthwaite Lake station I found a location from which to see the steam special on the lake shoreline by climbing a tree. I waited and waited, sustained by my sandwiches and a bottle of orange juice. There was no way of knowing if the special train was on time, or indeed running at all.

Unbeknown to me, such was the snowfall in the Manchester area that scheduled services were running late and public transport at a standstill. Many enthusiasts thought the trip would be cancelled. How it got clearance to run no one is quite clear, but it was if the 'Lakes & Fells Rail Tour' had Royal Train status and must run! With some spirited running by No 45596 *Bahamas* the special reached Hellifield in good time for *Flying Scotsman* to take over, but was then held for the Skipton snow ploughs, hauled by the two Standard Class 4s, to pass Hellifield and clear snow from the line ahead. When the train did depart behind No 4472 it was 54 minutes late, then came to a halt at Settle station as the snow ploughs had not cleared Ribblehead and Blea Moor signal box. However, a good climb of the 'Long Drag' saw *Flying Scotsman* speed through Garsdale, passing the snowplough engines that were taking water.

Meanwhile, freezing and half way up a tree by the side of Bassenthwaite Lake, I was unable to get down in case the train appeared. I had no way of knowing the latest situation. However, 80 minutes behind time the silence was broken by the sound of safety valves blowing off, as round the corner and skirting the lake came Ivatt Class 2 2-6-0s Nos 46426 and 46458. With the press of a finger I had that picture I had planned for all day.

It was now 4.30 on the Saturday afternoon at Bassenthwaite Lake station and I managed to catch the train to Keswick and on to Carlisle and home. This was not a day on the S&C for me, but thanks to the pictures of John Boyes, who battled with John Emmerson through the snow to reach Garsdale, readers can see the steam-hauled railtour on the S&C.

With the entire line from Penrith to Workington now lifted, the 'Lakes & Fells Rail Tour' that traversed the S&C can never be repeated. It was a day with vivid memories that all who ventured out in the snow will never forget.

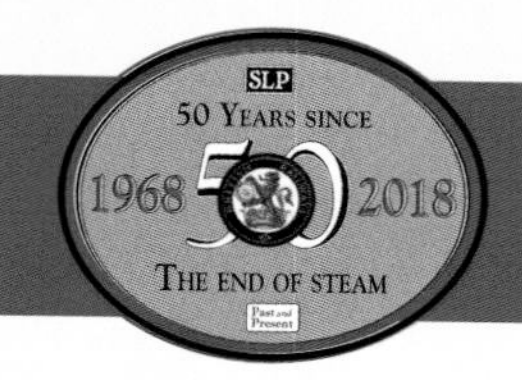

11. S&C STEAM STOPPING TRAINS NO MORE

The steam-hauled stopping trains between Carlisle and Hellifield were always looked out for when visiting the line because, unlike freight traffic, they ran to a firm timetable. There were two trains in each direction, stopping at all stations, but in the 1960s there were four more stations than today between Appleby and Carlisle – Little Salkeld, Culgaith, Newbiggin and Long Marton – all now closed. There were also stopping trains every morning and evening between Appleby and Carlisle, and the morning 07.12 from Garsdale to Skipton.

All the stations were staffed, which is quite remarkable considering the infrequency of trains, but that was normal in the 1960s, even for main lines or branch lines that made a loss. On the Settle & Carlisle line my pictures would indicate that the station staff had to produce their own departure timetables, with hand-written examples at Dent and Horton-in-Ribblesdale, whereas Kirkby Stephen West had a locally printed one. The latter station had perhaps the worst train service of all, with the first train to Carlisle at 13.12 – little wonder it could only offer a half-day excursion to Carlisle for 9s 6d. The 13.12 train was the return Kingmoor steam diagram to Hellifield that left Carlisle at 08.05 – it was as if the loco roster had greater importance than the passengers convenience!

I often used the stopping trains and well remember in particular being hauled by Ivatt 4MT No 43004 from Armathwaite to Carlisle, by Class 5 No 45075 from Kirkby Stephen West to Garsdale, and by BR Standard No 72008 *Clan Macleod* from Dent to Garsdale.

A well-kept oil lamp at Armathwaite station.

The motive power for the all-stations trains was provided by Kingmoor, with Class 5s being the norm, but as the end approached BR Standard 'Clan' or 'Britannia' 'Pacifics' were used. The normal motive power for the Appleby trains was an Ivatt 4MT from Kingmoor, and the 07.12 from Garsdale used a Standard Class 2 tank from Skipton shed.

Here are some images of the stations, timetables, people and trains that give a flavour of what the last years of steam passenger operation was like, before it ended in 1966.

Ivatt Class 4 2-6-0 No 43004 brings the 19.30 Appleby to Carlisle stopping train into Armathwaite station, then is seen later in the bay platform at Carlisle having arrived with the same train a few minutes before 20.36.

Class 5 No 44900 departs from Carlisle with the evening stopping train to Bradford Forster Square while on the right is Ivatt 2-6-0 No 46455 on station pilot duties.

This unusual view captures an unidentified Class 5 pulling away from Armathwaite station with the afternoon stopping train to Carlisle.

The poster advertising fares from Kirkby Stephen West makes interesting reading, especially as the first train to Carlisle was so late in the day at 13.12!

A rare picture inside the ticket office at Kirkby Stephen West sees the station master take a single to Garsdale out of the rack late at night in the winter of 1965.

In October 1966 the weather sums up the depressed state of the steam stopping train service. Neglected 'Britannia' 'Pacific' No 70042 *Lord Roberts* calls at Kirkby Stephen West with the morning three-coach stopping train to Hellifield.

In this unusual view at Kirkby Stephen West in August 1966, Class 5 No 44662 brings the 12.08 Hellifield to Carlisle stopping train into the station while on the left 'Jubilee' No 45593 *Kolhapur* shunts into the siding behind the goods shed with a mineral train to wait for a gap in the traffic to climb to Ais Gill.

BR Standard 'Clan' 'Pacific' No 72008 *Clan Macleod* prepares for departure from Garsdale with the 12.08 Hellifield to Carlisle stopping train on 17 July 1965.

A young boy from the nearby railway houses at Garsdale gets the driver's attention prior to Class 5 No 44828 departing for Carlisle in the spring of 1966.

Left: In November 1966 the only information for passengers at Dent was this handwritten piece of paper stuck in the window of the run-down station.

Below: Class 5 No 44667 brings the 12.08 Hellifield to Carlisle stopping train off Ribblehead Viaduct on a fine day in August 1966.

Left: In August 1965 the Horton-in-Ribblesdale timetable would appear to have been done by a steam enthusiast on the station staff.

Below: On a wet, misty day in October 1966 'Britannia' 'Pacific' No 70042 *Lord Roberts* brings the 12.08 Hellifield to Carlisle stopping train over the River Ribble near Stainforth.

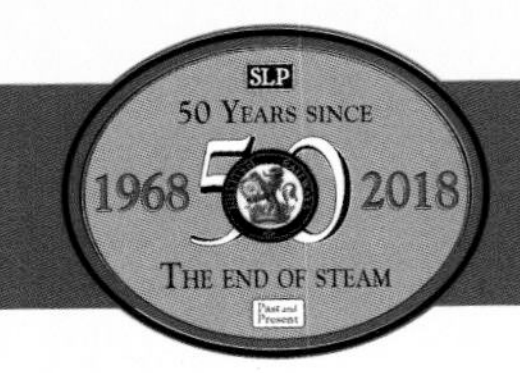

12. The final winter of BR steam on the S&C

The final winter to see steam working over the S&C was that of 1966/67, although we did not know that at the time. The amount of steam-hauled freights had diminished from only a few years earlier and, with limited daylight and the small number of trains, it was only by keeping in contact with the ever-helpful signalmen that we knew if there were any trains at all.

By now my sturdy Jack Taylor cycle, which had been my only mode of transport to reach the S&C, had been replaced by a ten year old Ford Consul, which I maintained myself, so I was now able to reach the line more easily. I cannot recall any days when there was snow on the ground and the sun was out; all my visits, which had to be on Saturdays, coincided with cold, damp days with sometimes sleet or snow showers.

However, the raw weather was soon forgotten when steam trains came into view, as the engines were often struggling with their heavy loads with huge exhausts that filled the sky.

Here are some images of the last winter of BR steam over the S&C.

The Ais Gill Summit sign stands out against the snow.

On a raw winter day in December 1966 Class 5 No 45204 climbs the last few yards to Ais Gill summit with a southbound freight.

A quick dash from the warmth of Ais Gill signal box captures Class 5 No 44781 heading over Ais Gill summit in December 1966.

Viewed from the road near Ais Gill summit, Standard 9F No 92249 brings the Long Meg minerals through the snow-covered landscape in December 1966.

On a bitterly cold day with frequent snow showers, Class 8F No 48351 battles against the wind as it climbs to Ais Gill summit with a southbound freight in January 1967.

Braving the elements this picture captures Class 5 No 45282 descending from Ais Gill summit with a northbound freight, also in January 1967.

'Beware of Trains', says the sign, when using the boarded crossing between platforms at Garsdale station, as Standard 9F No 92009 speeds through in a blizzard with the Long Meg minerals in January 1967.

Above: With snow clinging to walls and trees, Standard 9F No 92041 climbs towards Ais Gill Viaduct with the southbound Long Meg minerals in February 1967.

Descending from Blea Moor signal box, BR Standard Class 5 No 73006 has quite an unusual load – including an Army lorry – as it heads towards Ribblehead Viaduct in February 1967.

Right and below: The slow speed of Class 5 No 45426 hauling a heavy train of vans causes the exhaust to rise high in the air as the engine bursts from beneath the road bridge at Ais Gill summit in February 1967.

13. THE LAST ENGINE CLEANERS ON BR

It is hard to imagine today, with polished gleaming locomotives operating over the Settle & Carlisle line, what an appalling condition engines were in during the last years of BR steam – pictures in this book of 'Jubilees' *Newfoundland* and *Seychelles* show how dirty they were. Holbeck loco shed at Leeds and Kingmoor at Carlisle had long given up employing engine cleaners, as locomotives had a short time left before all going for scrap.

I had been introduced to cleaning engines before later photographing them by renowned photographer Paul Riley. My first attempt was not

An unusual location at Kirkby Stephen West catches two filthy 'Jubilees'. No 45593 *Kolhapur*, in the siding behind the goods shed on a long train of mineral wagons, is overtaken by classmate No 45626 *Seychelles* on the CTAC Gourock to Leicester express on a very wet August Saturday in 1965.

a humble shunter, but Gresley 'A4' 'Pacific' No 60027 *Merlin* at Perth in July 1965 (see the photograph in the Introduction). The shed staff, to my surprise, did not mind our activity – indeed, the shed foreman posed in front of his engine. We will never know what shed management really thought of what we were doing –after all, it was being done by enthusiasts who had no official permission to be on the locomotive shed and no permission to help themselves to oil, paraffin, rags and ladders. We climbed all over the locomotives, which were in steam, and had no safety briefing and wore no safety clothing – just everyday clothes and shoes. It is remarkable that such activity, which was common all over the UK, was allowed to happen – but it was!

I firmly believe that shed management had a lot of sympathy for this unofficial activity, as they, like the enthusiasts, knew that steam days were numbered and the engines chosen to be cleaned were frequently the last members of a class, allowing them to work their final days with some pride. This activity has such powerful memories of being so close to the engines in their last days, that words can not do justice to the situation, with Leeds Holbeck perhaps the fondest of all.

By early 1967 the number of ex-LMS 'Jubilees', which once totalled 190, was down to just five operating engines, so 185 were already in scrapyards waiting to be cut up. The last survivors were named *Alberta*, *Kolhapur*, *Sturdee*, *Hardy* and *Achilles*, and our group – dubbed the 'Master Neverers Association' (MNA) – cleaned all five at different times, making them look like new. But for these engines time was running out. By August 1967 the 'Jubilee' Class was down to just three, and on one special night they were all together in the roundhouse at Holbeck. It was well after midnight when we started cleaning the last survivors, finding buckets to mix oil and paraffin. Then using rags some would start on the boiler tops while others would do the cab and tenders. When all three engines were done, we reflected on the moment and tried our best to photograph them in the dimly lit shed – such powerful memories. After that night, within eight weeks *Alberta* and *Achilles* had been sold for scrap, and today the only survivor, to be bought direct from BR for preservation, is *Kolhapur*.

In addition to the five 'Jubilees' cleaned at Holbeck, many of them done several times in the summer of 1967, engine-cleaning was also carried out in the long sheds at Carlisle Kingmoor. Engines here were 9F No 92004 for the southbound Long Meg minerals, Ivatt 4MT No 43106 (now preserved on the Severn Valley Railway) for a freight to Langholm, No 43121 for the last steam to Alston, No 43049 for some of the last steam freights to Kirkby Stephen East, and finally 'Britannia' No 70013 *Oliver Cromwell* prior to working the last BR steam-hauled passenger train over Shap.

The unofficial cleaning of engines on British Railways was done in an age where common sense ruled, with no red tape and regulation, and the more relaxed attitude is best summed up three weeks before the end of BR steam when we were cleaning Nos 48773 and 45156 *Ayrshire Yeomanry* at Rose Grove shed for railtour duty. I was cleaning the top of No 45156's boiler when I noticed a police car approaching the shed, with its locomotives and 12 enthusiasts all over them. The two policemen got out of their Morris Minor and had a discussion between themselves as to what should they do. Meanwhile the enthusiasts carried on cleaning regardless! Realising that this could be a great photographic opportunity, I quickly got down from the boiler and very carefully walked in a long circular route, trying not to be noticed by the policemen. I eventually got right up to them without being noticed to take a unique picture of them looking at the unofficial engine-cleaning activity, which they just allowed to continue without saying one word. They too must have thought what harm were they really doing as the hours ticked by to the last steam on British Railways?

This bunch of hardy enthusiasts, whose average age was just 20, carried out their final cleaning session at Lostock Hall shed, Preston, on 3 August 1968, and a group photograph was taken. Many of those involved had already turned their interest to the steam preservation movement, many becoming loco owners themselves or holding senior positions in societies such as the NYMR, SVR and NELPG.

Reflecting on those far-off days of engine-cleaning, it produced some great photographs but perhaps something else far more important... The cleaning efforts raised the profile of steam generally and those engines that were about to be lost, and provided a boost to the preservation societies that were trying to raise funds to save particular engines that we now take for granted 50 years on.

Left: On a Saturday morning in May 1967 enthusiasts set about cleaning unique Class 5 No 44767, fitted with outside Stephenson valve gear, at Carnforth shed prior to it working a Morecambe to Leeds passenger train.

Below: The engine is later captured climbing Bentham bank with the train to Leeds.

'Jubilee' No 45675 *Hardy* was cleaned by the MNA gang at Holbeck for a freight to Heysham in April 1967. It is seen here running several hours late and making heavy weather of the climb through Giggleswick with a heavy load of vans.

'Jubilee' No 45593 *Kolhapur*, so filthy that its number plate could hardly be seen, has been relegated to freight duties and put in a siding behind the goods shed at Kirkby Stephen West to allow an express to pass through. Here it takes its load of wagons out of the siding and continues its journey to Leeds in August 1965.

No 45593 *Kolhapur* looks magnificent at 1.00am on that Saturday night having been cleaned by the 'MNA' engine cleaners from many parts of the UK.

After overnight cleaning, *Kolhapur* is seen a few hours later crossing the River Ribble on the approach to Helwith Bridge with the relief 'Thames-Clyde' in August 1967.

Above: The rewards of the cleaning session on 'Jubilee' No 45562 *Alberta* are clear in contrast to the two Fairburn tanks also in Holbeck shed.

Above: Enthusiasts turned their hands to making wooden replica nameplates to replace the brass originals removed by BR. Here is a fine example on 'Jubilee' No 45647 *Sturdee* in April 1967.

Right: No 45647 was cleaned overnight at Leeds Holbeck and fitted with a wooded replica nameplate, which can just be seen in this picture of the loco taken near Bell Busk between Skipton and Hellifield heading a coal train to Morecambe in March 1967.

One of the last cleaning sessions occurred at Rose Grove engine shed in July 1968 to clean Class 5 No 45156 *Ayrshire Yeomanry* prior to railtour duty. In the midst of the cleaning the police turned up, but the cleaners just continued! In our youth there was always the fear of being caught at an engine shed by the police, but with days to go before steam finished the police understood our motives. I secretly and quietly walked behind the police to take two unique pictures, with the officers totally unaware that they had been photographed.

The last ever regular scheduled steam hauled passenger train, that was not a enthusiast special, occurred on the evening of 3 August 1968. Class 5 No 45318, cleaned earlier and fitted with a simple headboard 'The End' makes ready to depart Preston station on the 21.25 Preston to Liverpool Exchange. It was a sad moment in history for those who loved travelling by steam.

The MNA cleaning gang pose for the last time on 4 August 1968 at Lostock Hall shed, Preston. The enthusiasts involved formed a great friendship that lasts to this day. On the running plate of 8F No 48476 are, left to right, Bob Clarke, Geoff Simpson, John Barnes, Dave Lacey, Dave Wilkinson, Ken Groundwater and Ian Krause. On the ground, left to right, are Jim Bodfish, Peter Proud, Kevin Gould, Dave Gouldthorpe, Tony Bending, Barry Buckfield, Neville Stead, Dave Williams and Mick York. The MNA are producing their own book: Never again - the complete works Details from mnabooks.com.

14. Last steam to Alston

The 'Beeching axe' had closed many branch lines in the north, but somehow the Alston branch survived the mid-1960s cuts due to the poor road network from Haltwhistle station on the Newcastle to Carlisle line. However, by 1967 the Branch was a shadow of its former self, with the steam loco shed and passenger train shed at Alston demolished. The service was operated by diesel multiple units on the 'one-engine-on-the-branch' principle.

Carlisle Kingmoor was one of the last steam sheds in 1967 and some clever planning by the Branch Line Society and the Stephen Locomotive Society saw them jointly run the 'Scottish Rambler No 6' railtour of 6 March 1967, which included a steam-hauled passenger train from Carlisle

Leaving the impressive Lambley Viaduct on 6 March 1967, Ivatt Class 4 No 43121 heads the 'Scottish Rambler No 6' railtour, the last standard-gauge steam train to Alston.

No 43121 climbs towards Alston near Sloggyford with the last BR steam train to Alston on 6 March 1967.

In a brief moment of sunshine No 43121 stands at Alston station - a shadow of its former self on 6 March 1967.

to Haltwhistle and the full Alston branch.

The steam motive power for the train was one of the Ivatt 4MT 2-6-0s allocated to Kingmoor, No 43121, and the special was to be the last time a steam passenger train would be run to Alston in the BR era. The engine needed to be fit for such an occasion, and an evening was spent at Kingmoor shed cleaning it. The weather on the day was wintry, to say the least. For the first picture at Lambley Viaduct there was a blizzard minutes before the train came, but fortunately it cleared just in time.

BR eventually closed the line in 1976, but it is good to know that thanks to the efforts of the South Tynedale Railway Preservation Society the line reopened in 1983 as a 2-foot narrow-gauge steam railway. The society has gone from strength to strength over the years, extending the line northwards to the impressive Slaggyford in 2017, and erected a new train shed at Alston station for the benefit of passengers.

This selection of images captures the last steam passenger train run by BR on that memorable day.

Below: With the railtour passengers disembarked the passenger coaches are propelled out of Alston station by No 43121 on 6 March 1967.

Below: The refurbished Alston station on 5 July 2018 operated as a narrow gauge (2 feet or 610mm) line, by the South Tynedale Railway.

15. Last steam freights from Carlisle to Kirkby Stephen East

At the north end of the Settle & Carlisle line, the towns of Appleby and Kirkby Stephen remarkably each had two stations, one for the Midland line, known as West, with an East station on the North Eastern Railway line. There must have been competition between the two stations, perhaps more for freight traffic than passengers. With Kirkby Stephen West goods yard being at the top of a hill some distance from the town the North Eastern certainly had the advantage, and in 1967 it still received considerable traffic. The North Eastern line over Stainmore Summit to Darlington joined the West Coast Main Line south of Penrith, and was closed in January 1962. At Appleby the West and East stations were very close together and signposts giving directions to each station were still in place five years after Appleby East closed.

Remarkably, five years after Appleby East station closed in January 1962 the direction sign still existed.

Under normal circumstances the entire Stainmore route would have been lifted, but as there was profitable freight traffic from the goods yard at Kirkby Stephen and nearby Hartley Quarry, in addition to supplies for the Army camp at Warcop, the line was retained from Appleby – with a link to the Midland line – to Hartley Quarry.

Motive power was provided by Carlisle Kingmoor in the form of Ivatt 4MTs, and when visiting the S&C the freight to Worcop and Kirkby Stephen was always an attraction. The last steam-hauled freights ran in the autumn of 1967, but the traffic continued, diesel-hauled, to Kirkby Stephen goods yard until 4 September 1971 and to Hartley Quarry until October 1974, when the line was cut back to Warcop. The Army continued to use the line until 1989.

Since the line fell into disuse, two heritage railways have been formed on the old North Eastern line. One, the Eden Valley Railway Trust, is based at Worcop, while the Stainmore Railway Company is based at the old Kirkby Stephen East, where considerable development has taken place with a refurbished station, new platforms and a locomotive shed, and in the long term a turntable will be installed. An undoubted highlight for the Stainmore Railway Company included a Stainmore 150 event in 2011, when a full-size replica Stainmore Summit sign was erected at the summit – the originals are in museums at Darlington and York – and Standard Class 2 No 78019 returned to Kirkby Stephen from where it once operated.

Included here are some images of BR steam past and present, highlighting that there are still railway operations, including passenger trains, at this location today, and well worth supporting.

At Appleby East signal box the signalman gives instructions to the crew of Ivatt Class 4 No 43121 as the Kirkby Stephen East freight passes through on its way back to Carlisle in August 1967.

Viewed from a nearby hilltop in January 1966 is Kirkby Stephen East station, which still exists today. Ivatt Class 4 No 43026 brings a lengthy load of mineral wagons for the goods yard and quarry past the closed station. Of interest are the tower on the bridge and the steps once used by passengers to reach the platforms, and the remains of the old steam shed on the extreme left.

Ivatt Class 4 No 43000 brings the Kirby Stephen freight under the footbridge that still exists today near the station, in September 1967. This engine received fame, with classmate No 43063, when it hauled the 'Wansbeck Piper' railtour from Newcastle to Woodburn on 30 October 1966.

From the footplate of Ivatt Class 4 No 43023, as the freight returns to Carlisle, the camera catches the view of the derelict Kirkby Stephen East station in January 1967; today it has been carefully restored by volunteers.

In the same scene 44 years later, on 27 August 2011, the station, now owned by the Stainmore Railway Company, is fully restored. A special Stainmore 150 event saw Standard Class 2 No 78019 return to Kirkby Stephen from where it once operated, and it is seen here departing with a passenger train. An earlier picture of the engine on shed is on page 16 in Chapter 1.

16. Off the beaten track

An adventurous spirit and a search for unusual photographic angles led to some interesting locations, whether on a rock ledge, climbing a tree or up a signal, with permission from the signalman. All these pictures from the last days of steam on British Railways are special memories in their own right. Now can you spot the locations without reading the captions?

One of the last operational Royal Scots No 46115 *Scots Guardsman* brings a mixed freight from Carlisle Kingmoor marshalling yards past Bog Junction on the line that avoids Carlisle station and is about to pass under the West Coast Main Line in August 1965. Note the number of chimneys on the skyline..

With its front number plate in need of a clean, Standard 9F No 92048 approaches Newbiggin, between Carlisle and Appleby, with a freight for Leeds in April 1965.

In the rock cutting between Settle Junction and Settle station, 'Jubilee' No 45660 *Rooke*, with excursion number 1S67 chalked on its smokebox, powers its train up the 'Long Drag' in July 1965.

After a torrential downpour the sun came out and I ran up the track from Horton-in-Ribblesdale station to capture absolutely filthy 'Jubilee' No 45626 *Seychelles* as it took a relief 'Thames-Clyde Express' from Leeds to Carlisle in August 1965.

Caught between the pine trees north of Armathwaite station is 'Jubilee' No 45593 *Kolhapur*, on a relief 'Thames-Clyde Express' in July 1965.

Class 5 No 44828 bring a northbound parcels train past Armathwaite signal box on its way to Leeds in July 1965.

An unusual view of Settle Junction catches Peppercorn 'A1' 'Pacific' No 60131 *Osprey* heading downhill with the CTAC Gourock to Leicester express in August 1965.

A location perhaps easier to spot is Horton-in-Ribblesdale station, where Standard 9F No 92009 drifts downhill with a mixed freight for Leeds in July 1965.

This view from the top of the water tank at Garsdale, long since removed, shows the station as it was in June 1966, as Class 5 No 44780 speeds through with a mixed freight to Leeds.

With the consent of the Dent signalman, this elevated view from the top of a signal catches Class 5 No 44689 passing the signal box with a northbound freight in June 1966. Note the rich mixture of freight being pulled, including vans, oil tanks and large steel pipes.

The windswept tree is a clue to the location as a Standard 9F, its number plate unreadable, steams past Blea Moor signal box on a raw day in March 1966.

Above: A fond location for many photographs today is Ais Gill Viaduct. Here 'Britannia' No 70035 *Rudyard Kipling* speeds towards the summit in fine style with an excursion in August 1967, with an enthusiast lucky enough to be getting a footplate ride.

Left: Viewed from a treetop, the safety valves of a Class 5 lift as it speeds downhill over Smardale Viaduct in September 1966.

Right: With the remains of snow fences in the foreground, this lovely early morning view brings out the curve of Arten Gill Viaduct as a Class 5 with a heavy load of vans heads for Leeds in August 1965.

In this busy scene at Horton-in-Ribblesdale signal box, the signalman has a word with the driver of 8F No 48160 as it heads a freight downhill, while on the left Standard No 75011 awaits the road up the bank to Ribblehead in August 1966.

The driver makes a backward glance at the photographer as his 8F No 48641 heads for Carlisle at Langwathby station, about to pass a Class 5 on a parcels train heading south on a wet March day in 1967.

At the very recognisable location of Ribblehead Viaduct, a struggling Class 5 on a heavy freight plods to the top of the climb and the easier grade though Dent in July 1967.

In August 1967 double-headed Class 8Fs plod across Ribblehead Viaduct with a 1,000-ton train of track panels for the West Coast Main Line upgrade prior to electrification.

Viewed from high up in a tree that still exists today near Blea Moor signal box, Carlisle Kingmoor's dirty Standard 9F No 92024, a former Crosti-boilered engine introduced in 1955 but later rebuilt as a standard boiler, comes off Ribblehead Viaduct with a Carlisle-bound freight in July 1965.

'Britannias' in trouble: two locos, Nos 70023 *Venus* and 70013 *Oliver Cromwell*, were travelling from Carlisle Kingmoor to Hellifield prior to double-heading a railtour on 4 June 1967 when they were put in a siding at Horton-in-Ribblesdale to allow an express to pass. In the process *Venus*'s front bogie became derailed. A third 'Britannia', No 70039 *Sir Christopher Wren*, was rushed from Carlisle to Hellifield to deputise.

Just north of Horton-in-Ribblesdale, where 'Britannias' *Oliver Cromwell* and *Venus* were stuck due to the derailment, their classmate No 70039 *Sir Christopher Wren*, , without front number plate or nameplates, hauls the LCGB 'Thames-Tyne Limited' railtour to Carlisle on 4 June 1967.

On a sunny March day in 1967, just south of Hellifield on the climb to Bell Busk, Standard 9F No 92077 pilots Class 5 No 44927 with an oil tank train from Heysham to Leeds.

Double-headed steam was rare on the S&C. However, in August 1967 track panel trains weighing in the order of 1,000 tons required two locomotives. Here two 8Fs, with No 48268 leading, approach Ais Gill Summit, no doubt with some relief for the fireman.

An unusual viewpoint captures Class 5 No 44973 crossing Ormside Viaduct, just south of Appleby, with a southbound freight in May 1966.

Crossing the River Eden at Ormside Viaduct, a 'Britannia' 'Pacific', with safety valves blowing, speeds downhill to Appleby with a Carlisle-bound freight in May 1966.

On 5 October 1967 the Stephenson Locomotive Society operated a 'Carlisle Kingmoor Limited' railtour with 'Britannia' No 70013 *Oliver Cromwell* as motive power. After stopping at Blea Moor signal box to regain steam pressure, the 'Britannia' restarts its train for Carlisle.

On 30 September 1967 the RCTS requested that the last 'Jubilee', No 45562 *Alberta*, be rostered on a freight to Carlisle and a brake van coupled next to the engine for its members. Here the train comes off Ribblehead Viaduct with many enthusiasts in the brake van enjoying the journey.

Viewed from high up on the fells, here is a different view of Ais Gill Viaduct with a 9F on the southbound Long Meg minerals in March 1967.

The short milk train from Appleby to Carlisle fits perfectly in this picture of Ivatt No 43039 on Long Marton Viaduct during July 1966.

'Jubilee' No 45697 *Achilles* looks in fine form as it climbs towards Selside with a Carlisle-bound express in early 1967. The green engine actually had a black tender borrowed from a Class 5 to keep it in traffic.

A track panel train of about 1,000 tons hauled by 8F No 48537 piloting a 9F slowly plods through Horton-in-Ribblesdale in August 1967.

On 7 October 1967 the last BR passenger train hauled by a 'Jubilee' ran over the Settle & Carlisle. No 45562 *Alberta* is hauling the 'South Yorkshireman' railtour round Smardale curve, luckily capturing the last rays of the sun.

Seeing regular 'Jubilee'-hauled passenger trains every Saturday over the S&C in the summer of 1967 was almost unbelievable so late in the days of BR steam, when 185 out of the 190 engines of the class had already been scrapped. Here on the a sunny Saturday in the last period of operation No 45593 *Kolhapur*, cleaned overnight at Holbeck by the MNA gang, is captured climbing away from Ribblehead with a Carlisle-bound express in late August 1967.

In August 1967 a double headed Class 8F's plod across Ribblehead viaduct with a 1,000 ton train of track panels for the West Coast Main Line upgrade prior to electrification. As can be seen the train was longer than Ribblehead viaduct.

Walking down to Mallerstang on a lovely spring day in March 1967 I was caught by surprise as 'Britannia' No 70014 *Iron Duke* appeared on a southbound excursion, with the fireman building up the fire for the last mile to Ais Gill Summit.

17. 1967: The first private main-line steam locomotives on the S&C

The events surrounding the operation of private locomotives on BR, at the same time that it was operating its own steam, is a subject that would fill a complete book. This chapter will do no more than scratch the surface of a fascinating seven-month period, when engines such as *Flying Scotsman*, *Sir Nigel Gresley* and *Clun Castle* went to Carlisle Kingmoor shed for coal and servicing but stood alongside more than 100 BR steam engines that were still in traffic six days a week.

The first preserved engine over the S&C was the A4 Locomotive Society's 'A4' No 4498 *Sir Nigel Gresley*, which after overhaul at Crewe Works worked over Shap northbound then south over the S&C, and is seen here on a damp 1 April 1967. Interestingly the freights before and after the special were hauled by BR steam still in service.

The honour of being the first privately owned steam engine to work a passenger train over the S&C fell to the A4 Locomotive Society's 'A4' 'Pacific' No 4498 *Sir Nigel Gresley* on 1 April 1967 during its inaugural run after preservation and overhaul at Crewe Works. I saw this train at Ais Gill summit, but what was different then was that the train ahead of No 4498 was BR Class 5 No 44767 on a short freight, and the train after it was BR 9F No 92009 on the Long Meg minerals. That was more than 50 years ago, and is an indication of how many years private locomotives have operated over the S&C.

Four months later another 'A4' traversed the route. Geoff Drury's No 60019 *Bittern* worked the 'A4 to Glasgow' railtour organised by the RCTS on 16 July 1967. This included a non-stop run from Skipton to Carlisle, taking water on Garsdale water troughs, and an incredible assent of the 'Long Drag', with Horton-in-Ribblesdale being passed at 60mph and Blea Moor box at 55mph, as there was then no speed limit on Ribblehead Viaduct. Before Armathwaite a maximum speed of 88mph was reached in a age when there was no maximum speed limit for steam. A month earlier a high speed had been reached with diesel power during the *Railway Magazine*'s 'Hadrian Flyer' railtour on 17 June; *Flying Scotsman* ran from King's Cross to Newcastle, with the return journey behind 'Deltic' No D9005 *The Prince of Wales's Own Regiment of Yorkshire* via the S&C. Descending from Ribblehead, the 'Deltic' is reported to have achieved 91mph passing Settle station!

On 16 July 1967 Geoff Drury's 'A4' No 60019 *Bittern* worked the RCTS's 'A4 to Glasgow' railtour. This included a non-stop Skipton to Carlisle run with high speeds throughout, and is seen hear near Stainforth doing nearly 60mph. With no speed restriction on Ribblehead Viaduct, it was passed at 55mph. The highest speed achieved beyond Appleby was 88mph.

The A4 Locomotive Society ran an 'A4 On Tour From Leeds' railtour on 27 August 1967, at a time when rumours were circulating that BR wanted to ban all private steam operation. No 4498 worked northbound for the first time over the S&C and returned to Leeds via Newcastle and York.

Encouraged by the threat of an entire steam ban for private steam locomotives, six railtours were hastily organised for a four-week period leading up to that total ban, as follows:

- 30 September: the A4 Locomotive Society organised a 'Splendour of Steam' railtour with 'Castle' Class No 7029 *Clun Castle* working northbound and Gresley 'A4' No 4498 *Sir Nigel Gresley* southbound.
- 1 October: a repeat of the 'Splendour of Steam' railtour with No 4498 northbound and No 7029 southbound.
- 14 October: for an LCGB 'Castle to Carlisle' railtour 'Castle' No 7029 went over Shap, was serviced at Carlisle Kingmoor, which was still full of BR steam locomotives, then worked south over the S&C.
- 28 October: 'The Moorlander' railtour saw 'A3' 'Pacific' No 4472 *Flying Scotsman* run northbound over Shap then south over the S&C.
- 28 October: the RCTS 'The Border Ltd' railtour with 'A4' No 4498 *Sir Nigel Gresley* worked over Shap northbound, then southbound over the S&C.
- 12 November: finally, billed as the last railtour before the BR steam ban from 1 December, the Manchester Rail Travel Society used Geoff Drury's 'A4' No 60019 *Bittern* to head 'The Mancunian' railtour, which included running from Leeds City through Skipton, Hellifield and Settle Junction to Carnforth.

BR subsequently announced that from 1

The A4 Locomotive Society ran an 'A4 On Tour From Leeds' railtour on 27 August 1967, and No 4498 is seen climbing away from Ribblehead towards Blea Moor with Ingleborough in the background.

December 1967 no more privately owned steam would be allowed to operate on its metals, the one exception being *Flying Scotsman*, which had a contract to operate for a little longer. The private loco owners could do nothing, and it brought to an abrupt end a short but fascinating period, enjoyed by enthusiasts and BR footplatemen, when BR steam operated alongside preserved locomotives. The Settle & Carlisle line therefore saw no steam railtours, even by BR locomotives, until the final BR steam train – 'The 15 Guinea Special' – on 11 August 1968.

Another A4 Locomotive Society railtour that was so popular it ran over two days was 'The Splendour of Steam', on 30 September and 1 October 1967. This is the first showing GWR No 7029 *Clun Castle* crossing a swollen River Ribble near Stainforth as it heads north to Carlisle on 30 september 1967.

In dreadful weather No 7029 battles against the elements through Kirkby Stephen with the return 'Splendour of Steam' railtour on 1 October.

Having earlier travelled over Shap with the LCGB's 'Castle to Carlisle' railtour, ex-GWR 'Castle' No 7029 *Clun Castle* is serviced at Carlisle Kingmoor prior to working south over the S&C on 14 October 1967. The picture captures the brief moment in time when highly polished preserved engines went to Kingmoor shed, which still contained lots of BR steam power. The shed closed ten weeks later and most of the BR engines went for scrap.

Another view at Carlisle Kingmoor on 14 October 1967 shows No 7029 *Clun Castle* with the unique Class 5 No 44767, fitted with Stephenson outside valve gear – the photographer would have been unaware that this engine would itself later be preserved.

On the beautiful evening of 14 October1967 *Clun Castle* brings the LCGB's 'Castle to Carlisle' railtour round Armathwaite curve.

Alan Pegler's Gresley 'A3' No 4472 *Flying Scotsman* with two tenders, having earlier worked over Shap, brings 'The Moorlander' railtour through Kirkby Stephen on 28 October. 1967

The very last preserved engine to run before the BR steam ban was introduced on 1 December 1967 was Geoff Drury's Gresley 'A4' No 60019 *Bittern*. Seen here on a wet 12 November, 1967 it brings 'The Mancunian' railtour through Bell Busk between Skipton and Hellifield. All preserved main-line engines then had a uncertain future, and steam was not to return to the S&C for more than ten years.

18. The last BR steam-hauled train: 11 August 1968

At the start of 1968 BR steam operation was still considerable, with 11 motive power depots involved, all in the North West of England. However, major cutbacks in May 1968 left only Carnforth, Rose Grove (Burnley) and Lostock Hall (Preston) as steam sheds, and a full detailed account of this period is described in the much acclaimed book *Steam: The Grand Finale* by Alan Castle.

In those final months BR steam was still working on freight and passenger traffic, and there were dozens of last steam specials all over the North West, but none were allowed over the Settle & Carlisle line.

BR steam's last stand could have been on a quiet backwater, but BR remarkably still needed steam power for some of its public passenger trains on the main lines. I was at Preston station on 3 August 1968 to see Class 5 No 45318 adorned with a headboard that said it all: 'The End'. After being photographed, it departed on the 21.25 Preston to Liverpool Exchange service, and as the sound of its exhaust faded as it climbed away and the last carriage tail light eventually disappeared an era had indeed come to an end.

That now left a final big weekend of railtours. The next day, Saturday 4 August, enthusiasts gathered at Lostock Hall shed, Preston, to do their final cleaning turn of all the rostered locomotives. But after that weekend of frantic activity it sunk home that there would be just one more train to photograph in my lifelong mission to capture the last days of steam on British Railways.

British Rail itself organised the last train, which ran from Liverpool to Carlisle, via the Settle & Carlisle line. Dubbed 'The 15 Guinea Special', it was billed as the last main-line steam passenger train in Britain and ran on Sunday 11 August.

The BR ticket for the last steam passenger train run by British Railways.

I had planned many trips to photograph steam, travelling at first by cycle, then later by car, and many of the results are recorded in this book – but how do you plan for the very last steam passenger train? I decided to first travel on the Saturday, the day before the special, to Carnforth to see 'Britannia' No 70013 *Oliver Cromwell* and check that it was cleaned and to take some last pictures – my favourite was one taken after dark viewed from the roof of Carnforth shed. Later that night the engine moved to Lostock Hall shed, then on to Manchester to pick up the special, diagrammed as IT57.

On the Sunday I opted to see the train solely on the Settle & Carlisle, at photographic locations that were my favourites. I wanted to enjoy the day and, as the special did not pass Blea Moor until 13.24, there was time to meet old friends

With just hours to go before its last working for British Railways, 'Britannia' 'Pacific' No 70013 *Oliver Cromwell* simmers on Carnforth shed on the evening of 10 August 1968, before travelling light engine to Manchester to pick up the last train.

in the Station Inn, Ribblehead, for a pint to commemorate the end of BR steam. These were special friends who had gone to great lengths to clean many engines in their final hours and take superb pictures that are intended to be brought together in book form as *Never Again* (from mnabooks.com). We posed for the last pictures together to mark the historic occasion and, as the pictures indicate, everyone was in fine spirits for such a sad occasion. This group of hardy souls, who named themselves the

With the last train not due till after 1.00pm, there was an opportunity for old friends to meet for a drink at the Station Inn, Ribblehead, to commemorate the end of the steam era on British Railways. Here a crowd of 'MNA' members, who used to clean engines on BR, pose for the camera; I am in the white shirt towards the right! *John Hunt*

'MNA', decided that they would meet at the Ribblehead pub every year on 11 August, a goal that has been achieved every year for the last 50 years.

It was while we were picture-taking and drinking ale that we heard a distant whistle, then two Class 5s, Nos 44871 and 44781, appeared travelling light engine to Carlisle prior to working the train from Carlisle over the Settle & Carlisle later in the day. This caught us by surprise, and I managed a picture of the engines crossing Ribblehead Viaduct – but it focused the mind. Time was passing and the special itself was on its way.

Approaching Selside, 'Britannia' No 70013 *Oliver Cromwell* heads north to Carlisle with IT57, the last BR steam train, on 11 August 1968. *Dave Rogers*

I drove down the valley beyond Selside and had difficulty in finding a parking place as there were so many people about, both enthusiasts and non-enthusiasts, wanting to witness the historic occasion. I found my spot where the line passes the magnificent 2,278-foot Pen-y- Ghent, but the scheduled time came and went – the train was running late. The weather was good, with patchy cloud and a clear sky. Would I be lucky and have sunshine on the last day? Then, running 34 minutes late, No 70013 came into view and looked fine – and the sun was out too!

While at the Station Inn, Ribblehead we were caught by surprise as the two Class 5s Nos 44871 and 44781 crossed Ribblehead Viaduct light engine to Carlisle in readiness for the return leg of the last train.

After the passing of *Oliver Cromwell* over Ribblehead viaduct everyone returned to their cars to drive to Ais Gill. This is the scene near the Station Inn, Ribblehead with the car on the left on the track from the viaduct.

Back at the car, it was nose-to-tail traffic as the convoy headed north. Everyone knew the special was very surprisingly scheduled to stop at Ais Gill Summit. Whether this was for press purposes, or for passengers to get out, using steps, and take pictures, no one knew, but everyone was heading for the same place – the summit. After joining the long line of cars beyond the Moorcock Inn, we all knew that we would not make

With photographers at every vantage point on the approach to Ribblehead station, 'Britannia' No 70013 *Oliver Cromwell* heads north to Carlisle with 'The 15 Guinea Special' on 11 August 1968. *Gavin Morrison*

This fascinating view from the overbridge at Dent station sees large crowds gather to see the last northbound steam train behind *Oliver Cromwell*. *Rodney Wildsmith*

Total gridlock on the road to Ais Gill summit, where *Oliver Cromwell* and its train made a brief photo stop.

it in time. Eventually the whole road became blocked. There was only one decision to make. Lock the car and run to the summit, and that was what everyone did. When I reached the bridge and looked down, there was No 70013 *Oliver Cromwell* surrounded by enthusiasts at every vantage point. Ais Gill signal box, where I had spent many a happy day in the past in the peace and quiet, was now a mass of people, with no apparent police presence. The train stopped at the summit for 13 minutes, from 14.20 to 14.33, then departed for Carlisle. After its departure, all the car drivers returned to their abandoned cars and it was some time before the traffic could move.

When 'The 15 Guinea Special' reached Carlisle the 'Britannia' was quickly detached and the two Class 5s, Nos 44871 and 44781,

Before the return last train there was time for further refreshments at the Temperance Hotel, Kirkby Stephen, before a dash to Ais Gill summit to take a last BR steam picture. *John Hunt.*

coupled up at the other end; this saw the stay at Carlisle reduced to 14 minutes. Now on time, the special departed, but as with *Oliver Cromwell* the leading engine carried no headboard or wreath to mark the occasion, just the simple train reporting number, 1T57, on a board mounted on the smokebox.

After refreshments with friends at the Temperance Hotel in Kirkby Stephen and another group picture, I headed for Ais Gill and the viaduct just down from the summit. There was quite a crowd, with cameras at the ready, and on that beautiful sunny evening we listened for the sound of steam exhausts. I had stood at the location many times, but perhaps this was historically the most important.

Round the corner of Mallerstang came the special, the two Class 5s in full command of the task and running exactly on time. In an all-too-quick moment the train had gone and some enthusiasts returned to their cars. I decided to stay with several others as we had heard that *Oliver Cromwell* was immediately travelling light engine from Carlisle to Diss for a new life as a preserved engine. As it came into view – a solitary engine – it hit home that this would be the last image I would take of a BR steam engine in action.

I returned to my car, packed away the cameras and drove down Wensleydale. During the journey home to Stockton-on-Tees I reflected on the passage of time over

This was the quite incredible scene at Ais Gill summit as 'The 15 Guinea Special' made a brief stop and enthusiasts were allowed to go where they pleased, all within sight of the signalman.

'The 15 Guinea Special', now hauled by Class 5s Nos 44871 and 44781, are captured in perfect evening light as they climb through Mallerstang and cross Ais Gill Viaduct on 11 August 1968.

the previous eight years; every Saturday I had been out with my camera, and now British Railways steam was no more and life would never be the same. I had visited the Settle & Carlisle line so many times since the occasion when I cycled 100 miles to see Kirkby Stephen West when I was 14 years old, but now eight years later, after 'The 15 Guinea Special', I thought I would never see steam over the Settle & Carlisle again.

My last picture of BR steam captures lonely 'Britannia' No 70013 *Oliver Cromwell*, dwarfed by the Mallerstang valley, travelling light engine across Ais Gill Viaduct en route for Diss and preservation as part of the National Collection. It was the end of an era – no one knew what the future held and whether main-line steam would ever return.

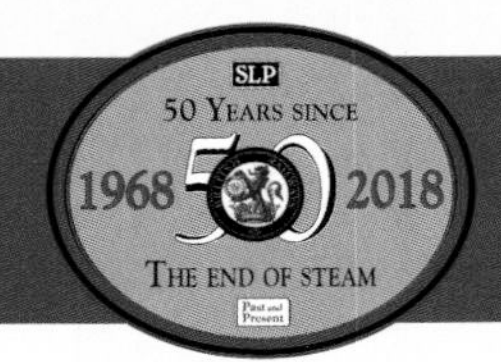

19. The triumphant return of steam to the S&C

Steam preservation history, from the 1968 steam ban up to the return of steam on the S&C, was a time of developments on a big scale, with new preserved lines such as the North Yorkshire Moors and Severn Valley railways being developed and the opening of the Keighley & Worth Valley Railway. The only operational main-line locomotive was *Flying Scotsman*, but after the NELPG's 'North Eastern' railtour of 29 June 1969 that locomotive went to America. I was fortunate to meet Alan Pegler at that time and show him the NELPG's newly purchased 'Q6'. He was such a great man, and one who should never be forgotten, for not only did he have the vision to save an 'A3' when the National Collection did not think it was important, but also showed that, with determination, running main-line steam could can be done. The main-line steam preservation movement will always be in his debt.

In addition to Alan Pegler, the preservation movement has seen many great people who have shown drive and determination for projects they were passionate about. At the end of steam in the North West in August 1968 one person who lived not far from Carnforth decided to buy the complete Carnforth motive power depot with the vision to run tourist trains to Ulverston and transverse the branch to Lakeside on Windermere. That person was Dr Peter Beet. He not only saved Carnforth loco shed, coaling plant and turntable from being demolished but was also instrumental in finding buyers for several Class 5s that today we all take for granted. With the help of many dozens of volunteers he turned the BR shed at Carnforth into the Steamtown Museum. Carnforth then became a Mecca for all enthusiasts. In addition to a fine display of locomotives, it had an excellent narrow-gauge steam railway and standard-gauge track for steam passenger rides. It also included Selside signal box, saved from the Settle & Carlisle line, and in its new home was made fully operational. Steamtown Museum also had an excellent museum of artefacts, a café and a picnic area. While external events subsequently determined that Steamtown and the Lakeside branch would go separate ways following a road scheme that cut off the branch, Steamtown

My chance meeting with Alan Pegler occurred while *Flying Scotsman*, on railtour duty, was being coaled at Tyne Dock loco shed. I invited him to see the engine that the NELPG had just preserved – North Eastern Railway-designed BR Class 'Q6' No 63395 – and he posed on the 'Q6' footplate.

The Beet family will always be associated with saving Carnforth shed. Here Peter Beet (left) and his son Chris pose on their Ivatt 2-6-0 No 46441 during a steam test at Carnforth on 4 April 1993. *John Cooper Smith*

thrived with annual attendances of 80,000 people. I had many dealings with Peter Beet leading up to the movement from Carnforth of LMS Class 5 No 44767, then owned by Brian Hollingsworth, prior to its movement to Thornaby for restoration by NELPG volunteers. During this and many other return visits in later years we always received full cooperation.

After two and a half years with no main-line steam in the UK, pressure on the British Railways Board saw the steam ban lifted on 2 October 1971 when GWR 'King' Class No 6000 *King George V* worked a train from Hereford.

It is hard to believe that in the early 1970s there was no national organising or regulating body for main-line steam because until then it had never been required. A key turning point was the Stockton & Darlington

Seven years after the 'The 15 Guinea Special' of 11 August 1968, public interest in the steam locomotive was as popular as ever, with 350,000 people witnessing the Grand Cavalcade during an event to mark the 150th Anniversary of the Stockton & Darlington Railway. In this amazing picture Standard Class 9F No 92220 *Evening Star* makes its way through the crowds watching the Cavalcade between Shildon and Heighington on 31 August 1975. *John Emerson*

Railway 150th Celebrations, which saw many engines move under their own power from all points in the UK to Shildon for the Grand Cavalcade in 1975. This event was witnessed by 350,000 people and was a major boost for steam. In the same year the Steam Locomotive Operators Association (SLOA) was formed, which brought together all steam loco owners to share information and provided a single body to negotiate with BR.

The SLOA started to run a limited number of railtours and it was only a matter of time before it was announced that steam was to return to the Settle & Carlisle line after an absence of ten years. 'The Norfolkman' railtour was hauled by Gresley 'V2' No 4772 *Green Arrow* and ran on 25 March 1978; this not only celebrated steam's return to the S&C, but was also a tribute to D.W. 'Bill' Harvey for his contribution to steam preservation. I was fortunate to meet Bill during the inspection of locomotives for the 1975 Cavalcade and we became good friends thereafter. Bill had helped to restore the 'V2', part of the National Collection, and taking it over the S&C was such a special day for him and all enthusiasts. The weather on that March day was as bad as it could be for such an important day, with strong winds and blizzards making photography difficult, but that did not matter. Steam was back on the S&C and, with talk of BR closing the Settle & Carlisle line, it was timely and a boost for generating much needed publicity.

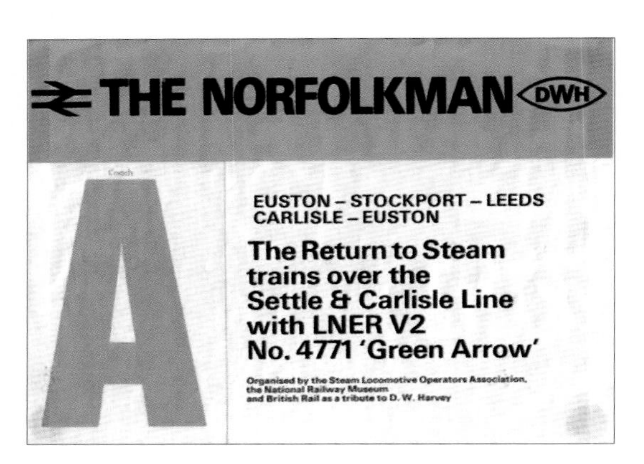
THE NORFOLKMAN DWH

A

EUSTON – STOCKPORT – LEEDS
CARLISLE – EUSTON

The Return to Steam trains over the Settle & Carlisle Line with LNER V2 No. 4771 'Green Arrow'

Organised by the Steam Locomotive Operators Association, the National Railway Museum and British Rail as a tribute to D. W. Harvey

Left: The Norfolkman' railtour of 25 March 1978 marked the return of steam to the Settle & Carlisle line. Note the BR symbol on the left and the initials 'DWH' within the LNER 'totem' on the right.

Right: Bill Harvey, who was responsible for preparing Gresley 'V2' No 4771 *Green Arrow* for the return of steam to the Settle & Carlisle line, poses on the footplate of North Eastern Railway-design Class 'J72' No 69023 *Joem*. Bill was a great friend, and the author of the excellent book *Steam Locomotive Restoration and Preservation*, a bible for early volunteer preservationists. He was made NELPG President for the help he gave the society.

Right: The weather on the Settle & Carlisle line is always unpredictable, and on the day of the return of steam to the route it was the most challenging for any photographer! This one was in the right spot to capture this image that sums up the day, showing 'V2' No 4771 *Green Arrow* battling against the wind and blizzard as it climbs through Helwith Bridge on its way to Carlisle with 'The Norfolkman' on 25 March 1978.
Gavin Morrison

Below: The return 'Norfolkman' on 27 March saw slightly better weather than its predecessor. *Green Arrow* looked and sounded incredible as it climbed the last yards to Ais Gill Summit.
Garth Mclean

After taking water at Garsdale, the 'V2' makes a fine sight as it crosses Arten Gill Viaduct with 'The Norfolkman' on 27 March. *Garth Mclean*

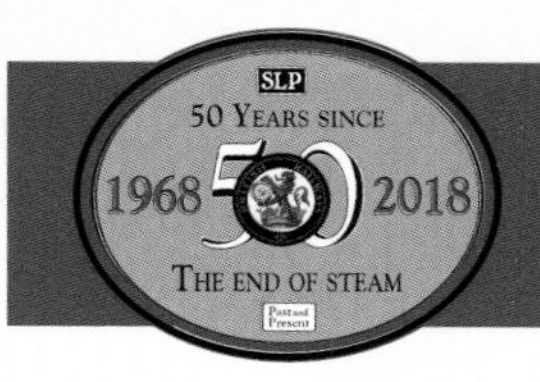

20. THE CHALLENGE OF MAIN-LINE STEAM LOCOMOTIVE MAINTENANCE

In the 1970s most locomotives operating on BR were doing so to some extent on the strength of their last BR overhaul in the 1960s, and mechanical and boiler inspections were undertaken by local BR inspectors from the steam age. Boiler insurance inspectors had rarely been inside a BR loco boiler, as BR did not need insurance – it was its own insurance company.

Now there was no Crewe, Swindon or Doncaster works for overhauls, and no money to pay for labour anyway – most restoration work was done by volunteers, who had to learn fast from BR boilersmiths or fitters. These early days led to a great swapping of information and I well remember, wearing my NELPG engineering hat, the many happy hours spent talking to Alun Rees, Ray Tranter, Graham Beddow and Richard Watkins of the SVR, Steve Allsop of the Bahamas Loco Society, Bob Meanley at Tyseley, and my old friend Bill Harvey. At that time few standards were enforced, but there was a lot of common sense based on BR experience. For example, 'A4' No 60019 *Bittern* was allowed to operate from Leeds to Glasgow with a cracked frame, but obviously kept under observation. Boiler tube suppliers were then plentiful in the UK and tubes lasted 10 years, while new locomotive tyres were supplied and fitted by British Steel in Rotherham. Today all these items are imported.

The formation of the Steam Locomotive Operators Association in 1975 brought all loco owners together, and by the 1980s engineering standards had been established under guidelines MT276. Main-line locomotive overhauls were still mostly done by volunteer groups doing their best to keep certain engines operational. By the 1990s loco groups had to deal with Inspectors based in Derby, with Colin Wood and Brian Penney doing mechanical exams and Sam Foster in charge of boiler inspections, and all became good friends of the preservation movement.

Time does not stand still and more complex boiler repairs – in particular the replacement of steel or copper tubeplates and fireboxes – have led to several good contractors being established to undertake this specialist work.

The cost of restoring engines to main-line condition today may well be in the order of £500,000, depending on what specialist contractor work is required. Taking a nostalgic look back to the early days, some great volunteer achievements saw so many engines return to the main line at low cost. One example was when the NELPG took on the restoration of Peppercorn 'A2' 'Pacific' No 60532 *Blue Peter*. The society launched an appeal to enthusiasts, who raised the entire restoration cost of £55,000. This low cost was due to the fact that all work, including boiler work, was done by volunteers.

Featured here are some pictures from the time when enthusiasts raised all the money and volunteers did all the work, and had the satisfaction of lighting the first fire…

The challenge of main-line steam overhauls rarely comes bigger than the full overhaul of LNER Peppercorn 'Pacific' No 60532 *Blue Peter*, which was overhauled entirely by NELPG volunteer effort. Here the overhaul commences with volunteers removing the boiler flue tubes at the ICI workshops on Teesside in 1989.

After hydraulically testing *Blue Peter*'s superheater header, it is carefully craned into position by NELPG volunteers Bill Brown and Dave Pearson.

During the *Blue Peter* overhaul at ICI, NELPG volunteers pose on the front of the loco during a Thursday evening working party in 1990. They include, on the loco, Chris Davidson, Bill Brown, Geoff Drury, Richard Pearson, Danny Forcett and Paul Hutchinson, and on the workshop floor Dave Pearson, Dave Farms, Bill Dobson, Steve Alder, Trevor Mussett, Mike Oliver, Dave Martin, Arthur Robinson and Bruce Pool.

Sam Foster, a popular man and friend of the preservation movement, was the chief boiler inspector for BR at Derby and responsible for passing all main-line engines as safe to run. He is seen here coming out of the smokebox of *Blue Peter* prior to its first steaming in December 1991.

The careful task of lining out *Blue Peter* is caught in this picture as NELPG volunteer Len Clarke applies the orange lining to the loco's tender in November 1991.

The undoubted highlight of any overhaul is lighting the first fire. Here a key person in the NELPG volunteer team, Dave Pearson, is given the honour of lighting the oily rags on a shovel and lowering them into the firebox to start the fire in *Blue Peter*. It was such a special and proud moment for all NELPG volunteers.

Right: With the 2,372-foot Ingleborough as a backcloth, BR Standard 9F No 92220 *Evening Star* comes off Ribblehead Viaduct while working the 'Border Venturer' railtour from Leeds to Carlisle on 13 May 1978.

Below: One of my all-time favourite engines over the S&C was Gresley LNER Class 'V2' No 4771 *Green Arrow*. She is seen here climbing towards Helwith Bridge with a northbound 'Cumbrian Mountain Express' on 25 July 1992.

National Railway Museum 'Duchess' No 46229 *Duchess of Hamilton*, having passed through Barran Wood Tunnels, south of Armathwaite, speeds along to Appleby with the 'Cumbrian Mountain Express' on 5 November 1983. The River Eden can be seen in the distance.

The system of operating over the S&C, starting with the Carnforth to Hellifield leg, continued for many years, but BR privatisation allowed more open access. A new railtour operator called 'Days Out', run by Mel Chamberlain, successfully organised the return of steam over Shap in September 1994 with the 'Shap trials' featuring 'A4' No 60007 *Sir Nigel Gresley*, BR Standard No 71000 *Duke of Gloucester* and No 46229 *Duchess of Hamilton*. This led to today's operations going over Shap in one direction and the S&C in the other, rather than using the Carnforth to Hellifield leg.

In those early days of main-line steam railtours, coaching stock was hired from BR, which had excursion stock at various cities in the UK waiting to be used. As this was progressively phased out by 1992 it was fortunate that other organisations took over the provision of excursion stock, maintained it and made it available for hire. These included Intercity Special Trains, Flying Scotsman Services, the Scottish Railway Preservation Society, West Coast Railways, Riviera Trains and Train Tours. Riviera Trains eventually bought the assets of Inter City and Flying Scotsman Services, while West Coast Railways also expanded its coaching fleet, and today Locomotive Services Ltd has joined coaching stock ownership.

The supply of qualified footplate crews to operate the vintage steam locomotives presented no problem in the 1970s and 1980s, with an abundance of steam men still working on BR. After privatisation of the railways the responsibility for allocating crews passed to Rail Express Systems. As steam men retired, firemen had to be passed out as drivers and this resulted in the David Ward initiative in 1992 when Standard tank No 80080 worked stopping trains from Carlisle to Kirkby Stephen.

A southbound 'Cumbrian Mountain Express' comprised of InterCity stock crosses the River Eden at the rarely photographed Ormside Viaduct just south of Appleby. The fireman on the Humberside Loco Group's Class 5 4-6-0 No 5305 is clearly preparing the fire for the climb ahead to Ais Gill summit.

On a perfect winter's day for steam photography, NRM-owned 'Duchess' No 46229 *Duchess of Hamilton* takes a northbound 'Cumbrian Mountain Express', consisting of blue and grey coaching stock, beneath Pen-y-Ghent on 27 February 1982.

On 20 February 1992 Flying Scotsman Services ran an unusual 'Cumbrian Mountain Express'. Departing from Bradford Foster Square, the train was steam-hauled all the way to Carlisle by Standard tank No 80080 hauling just six coaches. It is seen here departing from Skipton on its journey north; its movement to Carlisle was for driver and fireman training.

In the 40 years since steam returned to the S&C there has only been one period when steam stopping trains operated, and these were to train footplate crews. They ran for several weeks from Carlisle to Kirkby Stephen, stopping at every station, with a fare of just £10. Here Standard tank No 80080 departs from Langwathby with the afternoon train to Kirkby Stephen on 21 March 1983.

I can remember that many locomotive owners were worried whether steam would survive as footplate crews became fewer, and were in some cases less experienced. This was brought home to me personally when I found *Blue Peter* with its motion wrecked at Durham in October 1994, an incident that is fully detailed in the NELPG book *Keeping North Eastern Steam Alive*. Salvation came as part of the privatisation of BR and the formation of Train Operating Companies, which took over responsibilities for steam crews. West Coast Railways became the first privately owned company to obtain a Train Operating Company licence under privatisation, formed in 1998. From that date the company has supplied its own footplate crews and has now done so for 20 years, which interestingly is as long as British Railways did in the steam age. The other supplier of footplate crews today is the German-owned DB Cargo Ltd, which took over English, Welsh & Scottish Railways, although in time other Train Operating Companies may train footplate crews, which can only be good for the long-term operation of steam.

At Steamtown in the 1990s Bill McAlpine, who had a major share in Carnforth and at that time owned *Flying Scotsman*, sold his major share to David Smith. Due to the cost of maintenance of the shed buildings, the Steamtown museum closed at the end of 1997, the site then being used for locomotive and coach restoration. Many enthusiasts will have fond memories of Steamtown and its popular managers, George Hinchcliffe and Ian Atkinson.

With the absence of water columns, and Garsdale troughs having been removed in the late 1960s, the watering of the steam engines operating over the S&C became a problem. A dairy just south if Appleby was used initially, and the original water supply at Garsdale was restored by Steamtown, which took over responsibility for watering engines. One of the helpers was Bill Allan, who lived at Sedburgh. Because he was close to Garsdale, with the help of his two sons Andrew and Mark and supported by wife Ann, he took over responsibility for the Garsdale watering from 1983. The first engine they watered was for the NELPG's 'Cumbrian Mountain Pullman' railtour on 22 January 1983 hauled by 'K1' No 2005.

In the early days of steam operation, especially when the line was threatened with closure, Appleby and Garsdale boxes were 'switched out', as there were only two trains each way daily. In the early days there were photo stops for passengers, with Dent station a popular stop northbound and Ribblehead southbound.

National Collection Southern Railway 4-6-0 No 850 *Lord Nelson*, restored to working order at Steamtown, is caught in dramatic winter light during a photographic stop at Dent on 25 February 1984 while working a northbound 'Cumbrian Mountain Express'.

The announcement, after years of speculation, that British Rail intended to close the Settle & Carlisle route came as a body blow to rail enthusiasts, tourists and local people. The Friends of the Settle and Carlisle Line was formed in 1981 to save the line, while steam specials continued. It was a relief when the line was reprieved in 1989, and perhaps the steam railtours had made a contribution to the cause.

Because of the infrequency of traffic, photo run-pasts for passengers were possible. These took place at Garsdale and at Appleby for many years without problems. However, the increase in train services after the line was reprieved in 1989, as well as health and safety issues, meant that the run pasts were stopped.

The watering of engines still continued at Garsdale, but Bill Allan and his family retired from water duties in 2004 after 20 years assisting steam over the S&C, for which the preservation movement was most grateful. Amusingly, and without the Allan family

A rare visitor to the S&C on 7 April 1994 was the Eastleigh Railway Preservation Society's Southern Railway 'S15' 4-6-0 No 828. On this occasion it is seen performing a photographic run-past for the passengers on the 'Cumbrian Mountain Express'.

Viewed from the footbridge at Appleby station, LMS 4-6-2 No 46203 *Princess Margaret Rose* powers through the station on a photographic run-past for the benefit of railtour passengers on a southbound 'Cumbrian Mountain Express'. *Pam Marriner*

being aware, a special headboard, 'W. Allan and Co Garsdale', was fitted to Gresley 'V2' No 4772 *Green Arrow* on a northbound run to Garsdale, where it stopped for water. Needless to say, the family treasure that headboard to this day.

As steam specials became more regular, the Appleby Round Table launched an appeal to rebuild the station's water tower. This they did with the help of a local farmer, and it was brought back into operation in 1991. Today the locomotives take water at Hellifield and Appleby, and the once popular Garsdale stop is no more.

Right: Bill Allan (right) stands with his son Andrew with a cake and plaque at Garsdale station in recognitionof their hard work over 20 years.

Below: Without the family knowing, a special headboard 'W. Allan and Co Garsdale' was fitted to Gresley 'V2' No 4771 *Green Arrow*, and the train is seen here powering through Horton-in-Ribblesdale station.

Steam engine performance in the early days, especially on the rising gradients of the S&C, saw lots of enthusiasts with their heads out of the windows this was before a period when bars were fitted to windows following an accident. Of particular interest in the 1980s was the development of an unofficial contest that would catch the imagination of locomotive crews and owning groups alike, and as a result of which some of the finest ever sustained locomotive performances were recorded. The 'Blue Ribbon' – a name associated with the fastest Atlantic crossings – was born!

The names of the footplate crews are legendary – drivers such Willie Alexander, Willie Miln, Davy Gardener, Jack Eden, Kenny Stubs, and the Hayton brothers. They were backed up by skilful firemen, who later became drivers themselves – Brian Grierson, Gordon Hodgson and Paul Kane.

This unofficial contest was to see the fastest time from Appleby (milepost 265) to Ais Gill Summit. The locomotives in contention were *Sir Nigel Gresley*, *Duchess of Hamilton*, *Duke of Gloucester* and *Blue Peter*, which in the few years between 1991 and 1994 were all available. The top six fastest times were held by Nos 46229, 71000 and 60532, with No 46229 the winner with a time of 16.14 minutes and an average speed of 56.4mph.

For the *Blue Peter* attempt on 21 March 1993 I was on the footplate with driver Willie Alexander and fireman Paul Kane, and they were going for the record. With superb acceleration on leaving Appleby, as we approached Smardale Willie put a cloth over the speedo – we were going faster than the maximum speed allowed. With both injectors on, we were flying like the wind, but as we passed Kirkby Stephen Willie turned to me and said, 'I'm going to have to ease her back as the injectors are not keeping pace with water demand.' For normal operations the injector cone sizes were sufficient, but not for high-performance runs. This problem was not new, having been first raised by the Aberdeen shedmaster in the 1950s when *Blue Peter*, allocated to that shed, did performance tests on the heavy 'Aberdonian' service. While the crew did achieve 100mph with *Blue Peter* before Montrose, the injector cone size was an issue on the steep gradients. The Aberdeen shedmaster reported this to Doncaster Works, but nothing was changed. As a result, on the climb to Ais Gill *Blue Peter* achieved a creditable 17.33 minutes and an average speed of 52.1mph however, with an increase of just 2mm in the injector cone size it would certainly have beaten the 'Duchess' and taken the 'Blue Ribbon'.

In the cab of Peppercorn 'A2' 'Pacific' No 60532 *Blue Peter* fireman Paul Kane (left) and driver Willie Alexander pose for the camera before departure from Carlisle and an attempt at the 'Blue Ribbon' on 21 March 1992.

High-speed running was not the only highlight of the last 40 years, as there have been many 'one-off' events that in 1968 would have seemed unbelievable. The smallest engine to traverse the line was the Scottish Railway Preservation Society's North British Class 'J36' 0-6-0 No 673 *Maude*, pulling two Caledonian coaches to Rainhill in 1980. On one occasion there was a night-time running over the S&C by Gresley 'A4' No 60007 *Sir Nigel Gresley* to check the spark arrester system on a train called the 'Festive Firecracker'! Finally there was also a Royal Train, steam-hauled by 'Duchess' No 46233 *Duchess of Sutherland* with HRH Prince Charles travelling on the footplate for part of the journey over the Settle & Carlisle line.

Above: This is the fireman's view from the footplate of *Blue Peter* as it approaches Ais Gill Viaduct at more than 50 miles per hour on 21 March 1992.

On 20 June 1992 NELPG-restored No 60532 *Blue Peter* is seen climbing effortlessly to Ais Gill Summit on a southbound 'Cumbrian Mountain Express'. What the picture does not show was a request by the photographer to the author, seen in the cab, to make a dark exhaust; the loco was steaming so well it was not possible. *John Cooper-Smith*

The smallest tender engine to traverse the S&C in the preservation era is North British Railway Class 'J36' No 673 *Maude*. On its way to the 150th anniversary celebrations of the Liverpool & Manchester Railway at Rainhill, it had travelled from its home at Falkirk via the Glasgow & South Western line to Carlisle, then over the S&C. In this picture on 17 May 1980, hauling two Caledonian Railway coaches, it steams through Dent station.

On a freezing 12 December 1997 a special train, without fare-paying passengers, traversed the Settle & Carlisle at night in order to see if a new spark arresting system would work. As the only person at Horton-in-Ribblesdale, and unaware of when it was due, I used the phone on the platform that went direct to the signalman at Blea Moor signal box. He helpfully offered to phone back later with a message 'Just passed Settle Junction'. This enabled this most unusual picture to be taken at night of 'A4' No 60007 *Sir Nigel Gresley* climbing through the station.

A proud day for those responsible for 'Duchess' No 46233 *Duchess of Sutherland* was 22 March 2005. For the second time since being preserved the engine was on Royal Train duty taking HRH Prince Charles from Settle to Carlisle. The train also marked the 25th anniversary of the Friends of the Settle and Carlisle Line, who had done so much to save the line. Here, carrying a special headboard, *Duchess of Sutherland* powers through Kirkby Stephen with HRH Princes Charles on the footplate.

On 1 January 1994, against a dramatic sunset, LMS Class 5 No 4767 *George Stephenson* pilots 'Jubilee' No 45596 *Bahamas* on a northbound 'Cumbrian Mountain Express' speeding south and crossing the River Eden at Little Salkeld

In writing the previous paragraphs I have to pinch myself – did all those events really happen? In the last 40 years there has been a rich variety of steam power on the line, some of which we may never see again. Today we must be thankful for those volunteers and paid staff who toil in the workshops, those who finance the restoration projects, and the Train Operating Companies such as West Coast Railways that allow steam to operate on the main line. There are a lot of people from the past to the present to whom the steam preservation movement has to be thankful. We must never forget them all.